GROUNDED IN GRIT: TURN YOUR CHALLENGES INTO SUPERPOWERS

Grounded in Grit: Turn Your Challenges Into Superpowers

Copyright Lizbeth Meredith (2023)

All rights reserved. No part of this publication may be reproduced, stored in a retrieval system, or transmitted in any form or by any means without prior written consent of the publisher.

ISBN:

978-0-996959-69-8 e-book retail

978-0-996959-67-4 print

Published by PerSisters Press at L.A.Meredith, LLC

Cover Design JCOVERS Book Design

Dedication

To the inspiring clients and coworkers who've let me grow with them.

CONTENTS

Introduction
PART 1: Where You've Been

1: The Baggage We Carry

2: Stop Playing Whack-A-Mole and Create a Future of Your Choosing

3: What's Wrong With You? Trauma-Informed Care

4: Your Inheritance

5: Thinking Errors Balanced With Self-Compassion

PART II: Strong Communication

6: Communication Equation

    7: Assertive Communication Fundamentals

    8: Let's Put Those Skills in Writing: The Key to Holding Service Agencies and Government Service Providers Accountable

    9: Know What You Need, and Tell Your Community

PART III: Solid Community

10. Rupture and Repair

11: Fight Isolation and Diversify Your Resources

12: Decluttering the Friendship Closet and Curating the Support You Need

13: Aligning Your Values

PART IV: STUBBORN PERSISTENCE

14: The Crisis Makeover
  15: How Has the Journey Changed You?
  16. Final Thoughts
  17. Conclusion

Introduction

I've had a ridiculous number of awful things happen to me.

I'm not saying this to brag, or to be a trauma-comparer, if indeed that's a word. It's the truth. It used to be a source of great embarrassment. I'll give you a longer summary of the mishaps, because that's what you do when you write a personal development book. You prove to the reader why you're the right person to write it.

It was only after participating in discussions and events promoting my memoir that became the Lifetime TV movie, *Stolen By Their Father*, when I noticed how many questions focused on what helped me calm the chaos in my life and create a different future for me and my kids. Readers wanted to hear about resiliency, not catastrophe.

As a kidnapped child whose life was greatly impacted by domestic violence and abuse, sibling and parental alienation, maternal abandonment, poverty, and homelessness, I only knew I wanted better. So I grabbed the first hand that reached out to me, and *KERSPLAT!* Too soon into adulthood, I was married, a mother of two adorable little girls staying in a battered women's shelter, wondering how I'd managed to make all the same missteps I'd vowed to avoid. And then four years after the marriage ended, my daughters were abducted by their non-custodial father and taken out of the country to Greece. (You can read the longer story in *Pieces of Me: Rescuing My Kidnapped Daughters* published by She Writes Press in 2016.)

There was no simple or quick way to buck intergenerational patterns and craft a blueprint for a life of my choosing. Navigating college when both parents were high school dropouts to becoming the proud recipient of a graduate degree in psychology. Leaving food stamps and housing assistance behind after a stay at the battered women's shelter to owning my own little townhouse and traveling the big parts of the globe on my own. Parenting traumatized children whose kidnapping was a retaliatory measure for me leaving their violent father, to becoming a less hovering mom of two strong and educated women in their thirties who live life on their terms. Enjoying a three-decade career working alongside brave individuals and families in crisis who allowed me to be a part of their transformations.

So here it is. I've been through some rough stuff, then worked hard to change old patterns. Through the worst of experiences, I unearthed strengths and strategies that have improved both my personal and professional life. I've shared them with clients, and I believe you'll benefit from them, also.

But before Happily Enough Ever After, let me be honest, I made some mighty bad choices. The first was that I assumed my good wishes and intentions to be different than my family of origin would be enough.

Good intentions were *not* enough. And without proper examination of all I'd been through and how it had impacted me, without getting assistance to address and incorporate those experiences into my life, I jumped all in to make some big decisions. Like a marriage that had plenty of red flags visible to most, that would subsequently harm not just me and my daughters for decades but would affect so many people around us that it still boggles my mind.

To get to the life of our choosing, we often need to unpack the emotional baggage and decide how we want to re-pack for the life, and even adventures, we want.

I've long thought of my life as a story. It added a certain removal from the pain during tough times and provided a sense of detachment I needed to analyze what was necessary to move forward. My story, our stories, have a beginning, a middle, and an end.

We don't write the beginning of our stories. At birth, we don't ask for our set of parents. We inherit them. Yet our parents' mental and physical health, their race, profession, social standing, and relationship status, the country and even city they resided in, helped make up who we became. We don't choose our gender, yet it too impacts our access to reach success.

I bring this up because there are a host of popular memes promoted by primarily wealthy influencers, often with no educational background in the helping fields telling us otherwise.

Were you abused? *"We only tolerate abuse and disrespect from others at the same level we abuse and disrespect ourselves."*

Translation: *It's your fault.*

Have a goal? *"Feel as if it's happened and it will."*

Translation: *Positive thinking will make it so.*

Feeling overwhelmed, and wondering if your life has hope? *"The universe has your back."*

Translation: *Relax! Have more faith. Then all you want will come to you.*

That's not been my experience.

I don't think it's intentional. Perhaps based on this instant gratification world we live in, or a way to sell a product, these messages may not spark feelings of community or hope or a realistic view of the work ahead to create change.

I wrote this book for women recalibrating after life ruptures, even when that rupture happened long ago. I invite men to read it also. It's a blue-collar personal development approach. If you love reading Mel Robbins or Gabby Bernstein, this may not be your cup of tea.

Whether by abuse, a complicated divorce, or a different trauma that perfectly bisects your life, this little book is a hopeful one based on a collection of setbacks and the subsequent strengths gained in the process of enduring. Setbacks of mine. Setbacks in the lives of clients I've served. Setbacks I've created, sadly, for my own children, and had to go back and address. My graduate degree in psychology helped provide a foundation of information, and continuing professional education that supports evidence-based practices, combined with wisdom from coaches and writers featured on my podcast, and their own stories of persistence, provides inspiration.

This book is a response to the questions I get from women whose kids are now grown, or women who are retired and alone, now left to assess the collateral damage of hurts from the past, and sometimes are left to ponder the weight of their choices. I also hear from younger women in the throes of abuse or mired in child custody issues who're overwhelmed, sifting through a bunch of awful options that leave them emotionally hemorrhaging, and who want help dealing with the source of the bleed.

GROUNDED IN GRIT: TURN YOUR CHALLENGES INTO SUPERPOWERS

If your rupture is an old one, perhaps there was no help available. Or maybe there wasn't the awareness that trauma can nearly calcify inside the body, crystalizing to become a stone that weighs more over time than it did originally. Maybe you grew up in the 'bootstraps' generation, buying into the message that the quicker you 'just got over it' and thought more positively and repeated cheery messages, you'd be fine. After all, you've been the backbone of your family and friends, and the world seems to dole out extra credit when you bounce back in record speed and smile while serving others, munching on a diet of life's leftovers.

As women, we believe the message that if we take care of ourselves, crisis or no, we're selfish. If we don't complete our to-do list, we're failures. And if we don't take the temperature of the room, whether it's at work or at home, and ensure that everyone else is happy before we too can be, we're unworthy.

It gets old.

If you're living your life without regularly making it to the top five of your priority list, your life has already ruptured. It's time to respond. It's time to get scrappy.

If your life is also compounded by mental health or substance abuse concerns, I can say with certainty that nothing shy of everything is needed to tackle them and be successful. Treatment with a real professional, peer support, maybe even dietary and lifestyle changes. This book and the tools and techniques inside it are no substitute, but they can augment the interventions.

Life can be unfair. It is often painful. There are times when it feels like one giant obstacle course. I can't change that. I'm not writing this book to pretend that conjuring an easy path is possible if you would magically like yourself enough and repeat positive affirmations, again and again.

Your life is unique. Your impact on the world around you is immense, positive or negative. Everything that you do has a ripple effect on people you may not even realize are watching you.

I've learned from both personal and professional experience that when life gets hard, persistence matters. You may not have money. Influential friends. Innate talent. But if you're willing to bet on you, you can change your life, even if your circumstances remain the same.

I've also learned that it's entirely possible to turn your challenges into superpowers.

Recently, I stumbled upon a book written by a lawyer I met at a conference in the 90s when I was new-ish in my work as a domestic violence advocate.

Casey Gwinn was a prosecutor who firmly believed that intervening in violence in the home should be a priority for the criminal justice system. He is the co-writer with Chan Hellman of the book *Hope Rising: How the Science of HOPE Can Change Your Life*. In it, he wrote, "Hope is the belief that your future can be brighter and better than your past, and that you have a role to play in making it better."

Perfectly said.

I know your future can be brighter and better than your past. It's your job to use the tools and information in this book to help make it so.

And that's something I didn't do initially.

But as long as we are living, there are second chances. And thirds. And fourths.

So, if you're reading this book, there is still time for hope, and for transformation. Let's get started.

Resources:

Hope Rising: How the Science of Hope Can Change Your Life by Chan Hellman and Casey Guinn

The Body Keeps the Score: Brain, Mind, and Body in the Healing of Trauma by Besel van der Kolk, M.D.

ROADMAP

Everything I needed to know I learned struggling through college.

Well, not exactly, but it's pretty accurate. I give motivational talks to first generation college students about three lessons learned on that journey to encourage them through theirs.

The first lesson was to show up consistently for the goal I'd set. Doing something that no one close to me had done was no small feat. And what benefited me wasn't as much the course learning, but the irreplaceable skills gained during the struggle.

Arriving imperfectly to class, often late, homework incomplete, my clothes rumpled or dirty because I hadn't the resources to do better, took resolve and humility. There was no room for perfectionism. I simply could not break the vow I made to myself and my daughters.

The second lesson involved developing rapport in each class with at least one student or a professor. Not easy as a single, introverted mom taking care of kids on my own. Yet this added a layer of support, accountability, and enjoyment to showing up for the goal.

And the third lesson was to celebrate my efforts rather than the outcome. On a good day, I'm no Einstein. But back when I was getting my bachelor's degree, there were no good days to be had. My former husband was creeping around my apartment. Refusing to make child support payments. Calling public assistance and child protective services, claiming I was either living with an adult male or beating my children. Each claim necessitated a new investigation. To say this chaos often kept me from studying would be a gross understatement.

So, I learned to applaud my C's. I did mental cartwheels for B's and above. And I repeated classes when necessary to reach my goal.

And reach my goal, I did. Better yet, I now had a mini template that helped me survive hardships yet to come.

This book expands on those lessons, giving the tips and tactics to help tame trauma and calm chaos, so that goals become achievable.

I've broken it into four sections.

In the first, we'll look at where you've been. We know that before you can chart successfully where you want to go, you must know where you're at now, and how you got there.

In the second section, we'll talk about strong communication, why it matters, how to use it effectively, both in words and in writing, and red flags and personal hotspots to watch for to keep you in the safe zone with your words.

In the third section, we'll go over the importance of community. (FYI: nothing about my experiences has led me to believe independence is the ultimate goal.) But assessing your current support system, weeding out poisonous relationships, ensuring you have a voice and that you enjoy a good ratio of giving and taking, and cultivating your friendship garden is critical.

We'll not just talk about friends and family, but how to create a bridge with various agencies and organizations you may need to access to reach your goals.

And in the last section, we'll talk about the importance of stubborn persistence. You'll uncover possibilities rather than insurmountable barriers. You'll see how life's ruptures, whether it's a crisis, or circumstances that have always been tough, can refine you rather than define you, and why it's important to create new stress on purpose, and plan adventures of your choosing. And how you can bring the better, stronger you to the world and help others who are hoping to walk in your shoes.

Chapters will be short. I'll share things that have and haven't worked for me and clients I've served during my career. Please know that I'll try not to cite study after study throughout the entire book, but will list extra reading and resources, and reflections to consider that may be used as a journal prompt.

How to Use This Book and the Role of Writing in Your Journey

There's something amazing that happens when we can release our experiences to a page. It may not always feel good, but for me, writing my first book and subsequent essays reminded me that my life is a story to be shared. And what I didn't expect was that writing would make me re-think my perspective of people and events that had been hurtful.

A guiding principle in writing a memoir is to allow the arc of the writing to be informed by a time when you either grew from an experience or devolved and unraveled. That's what separates memoir from biography, where everything is covered. A good author will look for ways that sharing their story will benefit their readers.

In contrast, I want the writing you do for now to benefit you.

But let's say you've no interest in writing a book. Journaling is a terrific way to experience clarity, have an outlet for stress, and reduce anxiety. Reading it later can promote better learning.

Before you worry, thinking "I can barely write!" or "I'm dyslexic, no way," remember, you can choose to write simply as a journal. Or you can write a book without worrying about whether or not to publish it. Simply write. Don't worry about what anyone will think. Do it regularly, even if you only have five or ten minutes a day. It's an inexpensive and effective way to clear your mind and really honor both your experiences and your personal growth.

I'd love for you to be open to trying things you might not have tried before. The magic happens not by what I say or what any other professional says or does. It happens when you show up for you. Again, and again.

Once you've read the book and tried new strategies, you pick which ones you want to keep as a daily practice based on what feels right for you and will move you closer to your chosen destination.

Part I: Where You've Been

1. The Baggage We Carry

I was wrapping up a book event for my memoir a while back when a woman we'll call Beverly quietly took a seat in the back row and stared at the floor. It wasn't until I'd signed the very last book she approached. "Do you remember me?"

I did. I remembered meeting her a few times decades earlier. We had mutual friends. I remembered her for being someone who appeared to be so sad and so fragile.

Now, here she was, nearly twenty-five-plus years later, still looking so sad and so fragile.

For the next few minutes, she filled me in on the details of our gap years. "My husband ruled the house with an iron fist... I didn't leave because I knew what he was capable of... I worried what would happen to my children."

I'd heard that her husband died many years before. Yet as she spoke of him, she began trembling and crying. It was as though he was waiting outside in an idling car with a loaded pistol. Beverly asked if we could meet for coffee soon, and I agreed.

Two weeks later, I sat across the table from Beverly at a local restaurant while she wrung her hands, recalling the last two decades. After her husband died, she eventually met and moved in with another man, whom she later married. She never pursued counseling or group support. Never got an education or vocational training. Never made choices on her own. She was now underemployed. Racking up heavy debt, living above her means. And she couldn't understand why she'd spent her whole life reacting to the actions of others rather than making choices for herself.

I felt a swirl of emotions. Sad for her. Concerned by her passivity. Hopeful that it was not too late. Frustrated upon hearing that, she continued to sound like a victim in all of her other important relationships. After an hour, she came to the end of her story and took a breath.

"What should I do?" she asked.

"It depends. What are your goals?"

She looked puzzled. After deliberating for a few beats, Beverly said she'd like to become financially independent and increase her self-esteem.

I rattled off local resources that I knew were relevant and accessible, no matter her current financial reality. Nearly three decades of working in human services had paid off. "There's no easy road ahead. It's going to take a lot of work. You'll need to get out of your comfort zone if you want to break old patterns."

She continued to stare at me blankly, as though nothing computed. Finally, she shifted in her chair. "Can you write down the names of those agencies you mentioned to me?" she asked.

I could feel my eyes widen. It took everything I had in me to not rise out of my chair and leave.

"Here," I said, sliding a pen and paper toward her. "You write it down. This is serving your need, not mine."

Now it was Beverly whose eyes were wide. She was a smart and capable woman. The last thing I wanted to do was foster dependence on me by putting more effort into her goals than she did.

For the next thirty minutes, I sat with Beverly as she identified her priorities to get on track emotionally and financially. Together, we crafted a short- and long-term plan to address them. Just as I had done decades before as a domestic violence advocate and later as a probation officer, I nudged her to figure out what her goals were and to list the internal and external obstacles that would need addressing to reach them.

In contrast to Beverly, there was no shortage of women I'd worked with at the domestic abuse shelter who didn't wait until their husbands died to leave abuse behind. A few didn't survive leaving. Plenty more immediately met someone special within the first year.

Sometimes, I'd hear from clients who gave themselves time to heal. I didn't hear from them often, likely because their lives went on. But in the second category, the women who'd met another were gleeful to share their good fortune.

The conversations often went like this:

"Did you ever finish the support groups at the shelter?" The local domestic violence agency covered topics like self-care and safety planning in addition to providing a judgment-free zone to talk about our relationships, picking apart our decisions to leave or to stay.

There was no need, she'd say. She was done with a life of being abused, she'd say. Why autopsy her old relationship and listen to other people complain about theirs when she'd moved on? she'd say.

She was over it. Period. End of story. Why learn about subjects like how to get an order of protection when she would never need one again? Why bother with a class in assertive communication, or the impact of violence on children, or the one on positive self-talk? And the class on red flags of an abusive relationship? Irrelevant to her. She was just fine. She was living her happily ever after.

Yet when I'd run in to her a decade later, her narrative would change.

Her second husband was controlling, she'd complain. He'd kept tabs on her. She felt powerless. Again.

She felt victimized. Abandoned. Abused. And while she'd gotten preliminary information about abuse dynamics years before, she never followed through with steps toward recovery. She likely took a run at counseling, shied away from peer support, and hadn't developed job skills or even tried hobbies fitting of a worthwhile life. Sometimes, she shifted her dependency to one friend. One sibling. One substance. Now, all of her life's goals appeared out of reach. And she wondered why.

It's always easier to gloss over really tough times and grab on to the next shiny object rather than electing to swim upstream in pursuit of growth and healing. We want to put tough times behind us. We don't want to "dwell on the negative," since we'd never asked for our lives to be interrupted. We just want to get on with it.

It takes focus and energy and support to get un-stuck. And sometimes, it takes a virtual rap on the head to realize we need to.

Mine came in 1990. I was a twenty-five-year-old, holding my baby and wrestling to maintain control of my two-year old daughter as we stood in line to apply for public assistance. Our hair was mussed, clothes, a bit dirty. We were staying in the domestic abuse crisis shelter, and I had a protective order in place against my then-husband, the father of my children.

My world was ending, or so I thought.

"Ma'am, have you considered going back to college and finishing your degree?" the eligibility technician asked me toward the end of our meeting. She'd seen on my paperwork that I had earned several credits already.

I was incredulous. I told her it would take three more years of studies. "I'd be *28* by then."

She softened. "I hate to break it to you, but how old do you think you'll be in three years if you don't finish?"

She was right.

It would be nothing but an uphill battle to add college to my to-do list, given I was homeless, had no family close by to watch the kids, had no parental role models who'd attended college before me, and would be stalked not for months, but years, by my former husband. But to pretend that things would magically improve on their own, and that I couldn't endure the slog because I would be too old?

Absurd.

I could do hard things if they'd pay off for a better future. So can you.

My question for you: Have you had gentle or not-so-gentle nudges from a friend or stranger to do something that would require a big investment of time, emotions, or other resources you doubted you had access to?

How did you respond?

And on reflection, how do you feel about how you responded?

Yes, Privilege is a Thing

GROUNDED IN GRIT: TURN YOUR CHALLENGES INTO SUPERPOWERS

It also takes a lot of hard work, no matter who you are, no matter where you're coming from. A lot of hard work—and a lot of help.

"I wish I had received as much support as you did," a fellow abuse survivor I connected with said a few years ago.

"Do you think you'd have such good luck getting help if you were unattractive?" asked a male stranger I'd sought help from while recovering my kidnapped daughters.

Lucky? *Me?*

My life was at an all-time low. It was 1995. I was thirty years old then, temporarily housed in Athens, Greece. My little girls, taken by their non-custodial father against a court order four years after I left him, were living in hiding. Their father did this as a final act of revenge, payback for having left him. And now I–along with generous people across the globe—had done everything but panhandle on the streets to afford the airfare and lodging in Greece on my $10-an-hour job in to reunite with my girls.

Did I mention that even before I married, my family of origin that I knew then was in tatters, and weren't in the position to help me reunite with my daughters? Yep. Part of my first book. So, when the man suggested I was lucky, I wasn't feeling it.

I can't remember what I said in response. But I do remember that his words stopped me in my tracks.

My life felt anything but charmed.

Years later, when the crisis resolved and my daughters were safely home, I would think about his words. Because even if I had been through a lot, I still had advantages over others. Even I had privilege.

I was young. I was white. I was healthy. I was born in a first-world country. Apparently, I wasn't ugly. I wasn't addicted to substances, nor were my mental health issues so great that they ruined my efforts, though they definitely impeded them. And since I'd already been native to the land of chaos even before I married my former husband, I was familiar with managing adversity.

Recently, I saw a commercial about Southern New Hampshire University that reinforced this. "Everyone has talent, but opportunity is unevenly distributed." Grossly paraphrased, but you get the gist of it.

As a heterosexual, Caucasian American, even when I was at the height of broke, I still had greater access to things like grants, college and housing, all building blocks to later success. Racism, sexism, homophobia, and other forms of discriminations remain barriers to getting needed support to make big changes. There's no way around it. I believe that this book will provide value by giving tools to hold people and systems accountable on the path to equity. But that doesn't diminish the unfairness.

Support and resources had never magically fallen into my lap. There was no formula I'd stumbled upon that taught me how to ask for and receive help or know where to even look for it.

I continued to give talks at conferences and civic groups, occasionally flying cross-country to universities or bookstores. It had taken me two decades to write the story of my life, and I poured my heart and money I didn't have into its creation. Still, readers were unsatisfied.

GROUNDED IN GRIT: TURN YOUR CHALLENGES INTO SUPERPOWERS

"But *how* did you get through it all?" they asked at nearly every event.

The Imperfect Journey Toward Healing

At the women's shelter, I learned something that applies to so many of our struggles: leaving abuse was an incident. That's it. Healing from abuse was a journey. A process. Not a catchy formula given on social media or in a book.

Healing takes real progress that can't be accomplished with Cliff Notes. And the same can be said, for example, of getting sober. Getting sober isn't merely the absence of drinking or using. It's a process of reaching out for support. Learning how to sustain a support network, and actively seeking opportunities to give back to others who need it when the time is right. Finding alternate activities. Sometimes focusing on one day at a time. It's the desire for a transformation, not a quick fix to feel good enough. It requires a system of tools and support to create lasting change.

Speaking of getting sober, I need to mention that if you've got substance abuse or acute mental health or traumas that actively impact your life and aren't being managed by you with a professional, that needs to change, pronto, please.

But back to me. By the time my former husband kidnapped our little girls, then four and six years old, he and I had been apart for four years. I was still in my twenties but had already logged countless hours in counseling. My kids had done play therapy before they were old enough for pre-school. "Don't worry about it," people told me then. "You're so fortunate. They'll never remember what happened when they were little. It won't impact them."

And I half-believed it. I needed to believe it. The list of things I prayed they wouldn't remember included being exposed prenatally to the volatile relationship I had with their father. Witnessing physical violence. Bouts of my depression and anxiety. Poverty, once I left their father. Homelessness soon afterward.

But I did my due diligence and got them the resources they might need to heal, just in case.

Ensuring that children have the resources they need to heal and thrive was unfamiliar territory. In my family of origin, complete with a no- chance-to-finish-high-school set of parents, you shut up when bad things happened. Whether it was extreme physical abuse, witnessing family violence, dramatic divorces, a house fire, there was no permission given to name the dysfunction or to reach out for help.

And now, despite my efforts to do different, to be different, my little girls were abducted and taken out of country, which left me with the insurmountable task of navigating local and foreign governments, law enforcement systems operating in a foreign language, and traveling repeatedly across the globe.

Just over two years after the abduction, I successfully brought them home. Not easily. Not alone. And not without significant consequences. Yet I had no idea that the real work was yet to come.

Today, my daughters are strong-minded women. They've broken the family mold of early marriage and pregnancies. They love animals and the outdoors and travel. Most importantly, they're nice humans. They have plenty of emotional scar tissue from all they've endured, but they are strong and fierce and continue to show up for their lives.

Let me be clear: my daughters and I are still works in progress. While we've made great strides toward wholeness, perfection is nowhere in sight. We've put the fun in dysfunction and have the tools to deal with life's lowlights while making room and creating new highlights.

Resources:

Pieces of Me: Rescuing My Kidnapped Daughters by Lizbeth Meredith (She Writes Press, 2016)

Stolen By Their Father (Lifetime Television, produced by Cineflix)

Reflection

Has there been a single moment or a long-term event that has bisected your life? There was life before X happened and life after. What was it?

What hopes or goals did it cause you to question or give up entirely?

Which ones are worth reviving? Or how did the event morph into something good?

2. Stop Playing Whack-A-Mole and Create a Future of Your Choosing

Have you ever felt like your life was suspended in misery or chaos while everyone else's continued happily around you? Like you were a human whack-a-mole, lying in wait with a mallet to punch down the next problem that cropped up?

Whether you were a victim of crime, or went through a painful divorce, had a disease, or lived a life filled with more downs than ups, you can't seem to move through it and get on track to find a life you're passionate about, the one you will take pride in living. Somehow, you got stuck.

It makes me think of oversized carry-on luggage. We try squashing it into the overhead bin on the airplane or sliding it under our seat, but it doesn't fit. Inattention to our carry-on's weight is both preventable and costly. Retaining too much emotional baggage is the same way. It creates a hazard moving forward.

So why do we do it? Why do we continue to flounder when crisis management and the pursuit of healing after trauma or hardships is a skill each of us will need to master in our lifetimes?

I have a theory.

As women, we've been given the message that our job is to put everyone else's needs first. We're taught to apologize for having kids who might interfere with our professional world. Then apologize for letting work get in the way of our perfect parenting world. And if we dared not to work outside the home? We needed to apologize for not supplementing the family economy.

We can't win. Many of us survey a room of loved ones to decide whether we can be happy only after we've made sure they're happy first. Our parents, our partners, our kids, our coworkers. After we've cared for all of them, there's not a lot of energy left.

There is a time when putting the needs of minor children, partners, and family above our own are both necessary and sacred. But there's a time to take care of ourselves first.

When I decided I was ready to change, I had a vision for the life I wanted, but no idea how to get there.

Call a stranger on a hotline? *Who, me?*

Get on a waitlist for services? *It would take too long.*

See a therapist to help deal with stress during rough times? *What? I'm not crazy. Anyone under these circumstances would be a little nuts. Right?*

Attend a peer group or join an online forum to give and receive support? *No. I already know what they'll tell me*, or *I'm too busy*, or *I'm an introvert*. Or *I can't relate to these people.*

I used to want to hide the fact that my life read like a Greek tragedy. Some of us have had our share of travails, and someone else's too. I had to get over my self-consciousness and ego that threatened to hold me back.

And then I tried calling that hotline. I got on waitlists for services for every kind of help. I embraced a recovery model rather than simply changing circumstances. Years later, I read about the 10,000-hour rule author Malcolm Gladwell identified in his book, *Outliers*. His principle is that if one logs enough time, they will master a chosen skill or become an expert in their designated field. While I might not have hit 10,000 hours of crisis management, it's close. Because after working as a domestic violence advocate and child abuse investigator, I elected to work in a job where the mission was prevention of crime combined with victims' services, a juvenile probation officer.

As a domestic violence advocate, I was trained to not question the client's stories, to believe her, to provide information and support and safety planning so the survivor was empowered to make her own best decision about her relationship.

My next role as a child abuse investigator was a huge contrast. I learned to take nothing at face value. To evaluate statements made by those interviewed alongside evidence gained from collateral contacts. And to make a definitive plan of action to address abusive behaviors when appropriate.

And the probation work I landed on for two decades after that? It demanded the skills of a victim's advocate, an investigator, and a case manager. A perfect blending. As I trained for the job through my college internship, working first with adult offenders, I was schooled in thinking errors or cognitive distortions. I had so many of my own that I'd not realized how they'd held me back.

Now, I've long-lived my life through a bifocal lens of both consumer and facilitator of rehabilitative services to create change. Working for a busy non-profit and state government after my life was upturned changed everything. Bitterness about how things should have gone largely evaporated. Views that government inefficiencies were personal vendettas against myself and my family changed once I understood that demand for help always exceeds the supply.

GROUNDED IN GRIT: TURN YOUR CHALLENGES INTO SUPERPOWERS

I used that blending of what I learned at work—validate, investigate, motivate—to aid when the next crisis came, whether it was my client's or my own.

Like when my daughters were victims of a random violent crime, fifteen years after returning to Alaska from Greece. Or when our family needed acute mental health services. When life had to be rebuilt, again and again as the long-term impact of excessive trauma came to roost in my daughters' young adulthood. But I also brought what I learned from personal experiences to work to teach survivors of crime and families who needed support how to best access services and hold inefficient systems to account. Each emergency became a way to learn a new system, meet new people I never even knew I'd one day cherish, and provide referrals for the next parent at work or in my own life who wanted similar help.

When I dug deep and thought about what I'd most want to share, it all began with a commitment to breaking old cycles. We start with accountability. To our support system. To the agencies that serve us. Most importantly, to ourselves.

I titled the book Grounded in Grit because being grounded refers to staying calm and connected to oneself, even in the face of adversity. And sometimes it's in the midst of that adversity that we find the beauty of how it's shaped us.

***

A few years ago, I was asked to give a talk to the International Association of Women Police. "Tell them why you went to work in the very systems that failed you... that's different," the organizer said.

Which got me thinking, what would my life have been like had I not gone to work in the system that'd failed me? And had those systems really failed me, or had I merely expected too much of them to begin with?

If there was an advantage to working in trauma and crises after my own, it was to get perspective. So many of the juvenile delinquents and crime victims I've worked with had lives that were so rife with tragedy that it made mine look like child's play.

Often, they lived out the history inherited from earlier generations. But now and then, one would dare to swim against the tide and inch toward a life of their choosing.

You know how it's automatic to make an initial call for help after an emergency? For example, let's say you're having sudden crushing chest pains. Most of us would call 911 and get to the nearest hospital.

But down the road, when we're back at home and out of the danger zone, it's easy to want to just put the memory behind us. So, when we're told to change our diet, see a professional to address stress management, perhaps stop smoking, or begin a new exercise routine, how many of us would stay with this daunting list for more than two months? How about six months? How many of us would be willing to push back against our feelings of impatience, overwhelm, and anxiety to make permanent changes that may transform our life? How many of us are really willing to stay focused on change, even if it requires examining old thoughts and beliefs and habits, and get honest about what we can and can't change to live a life we're proud of?

It's easier to show up well when we are forced, when there are fires to be put out, when the stakes are high. But what about when life returns to a more even keel? Do we keep up good habits we may have employed during a crisis?

"But I'm just not as motivated as you," I've had friends tell me when I put on my ice grippers during lunch hour to begin my walk in the dark, 15-degree Alaskan winter.

Here's the truth, my friend: Motivation isn't driving my behavior any longer. If I ever wake up and say, "I can't wait to eat my leafy greens and get started on a walk!" please check my temperature. That's not my normal. But, around the same time I learned that you could love someone who is horrible for you and to you and still choose not to be with that person, I also realized that as someone prone to anxiety and depression, I must choose to do things because I know they're beneficial to my health and well-being. Even when they don't sound delicious or fun.

"It doesn't matter if you're motivated," extreme weightlifter Kathryn Bennett told me in a phone interview for my podcast. "You don't have to want to do it."

Her own journey with mental illness and addiction led her to get treatment, but she needed more than the standard interventions. She explained that so often, popular treatments require a lot of sitting quietly and focusing on thoughts. And her brain was simply too busy. "That was part of the reason I used," she said. "To calm down my fast-moving brain." Bennett's sponsor through Alcoholics Anonymous encouraged her to add extra stress to her life, to do something challenging.

Today, Kathryn Bennett is a nationally acclaimed weightlifter.

"You don't have to want to do it," Bennett emphasized... "I build my resiliency not through motivation, but through discipline... Do the next right thing. Just put your shoes on."

Life is easier when you're clearing a path to a target rather than punching down a problem, only to see another arise. When you're not running from crisis to crisis. But it's hard to stay on track if you don't first take baby steps and commit to habits and disciplines that will propel you forward.

You deserve to have support as you make big changes in your life. Maybe you're wading through circumstances you never would have chosen. Whatever it is, you don't have to go through it alone. I'm next to you, ready to help you cross the bridge if you're ready and want to change your destination.

You will need a vision for how you want your life to look. You will need to roll up your sleeves and show up, even when, maybe especially when, you don't feel like it. You must be open to new ideas, information, and feedback. It won't be quick, and it won't be easy. But you'll have the confidence to face whatever comes next, knowing you've pursued emotional fitness not for the sprint, but for the marathon ahead.

First Lady Eleanor Roosevelt once said, "You gain strength, courage, and confidence by every experience in which you really stop to look fear in the face. You are able to say to yourself, 'I lived through this horror. I can take anything that comes along.'"

I couldn't agree more, so long as we're intentional about how we move through the fear.

Knowing where we want to go is key in setting our internal GPS.

GROUNDED IN GRIT: TURN YOUR CHALLENGES INTO SUPERPOWERS

I'd never actually used a GPS until I moved across country by myself from Alaska to Tennessee in late 2021 and began driving on the interstate. I soon learned that you could set a GPS to avoid interstates. You can decide how fast or slow you'd like to arrive at your destination. But without knowing where you're starting from and precisely where you want to end up, all of that is useless.

One day this summer, on my way to my second paddle-boarding lesson in downtown Chattanooga, a sudden fiber optics outage interrupted my GPS service. Though a week before I'd arrived successfully and a few minutes early, now I floundered. I pulled over and called the instructor for directions.

"Where are you?" she asked. I looked around but couldn't find signs. "Close, I think," was all I could answer.

"I can't help you if you don't know where you are," she said exasperated. "Haven't you been here before?"

Ouch. But it made sense. How did I expect her to assist if I didn't even know my starting point?

You also must know your starting point. And you'll need a vision for how you want your life to be. That image, kept front and center in your mind, will refuel your intentions when you're running on empty to do the work to get there.

Resources:

Outliers by Malcolm Gladwell: the Story of Success, New York: Little, Brown, and Company, 2008

Persistence U Podcast with Lizbeth. Episode 28. Kathryn Bennett on When Typical Substance Abuse Training Wasn't Enough

Reflection

Give yourself five minutes of quiet, with no TV, radio, or social media. If you've more time than that, take it! Take an objective look at your life currently.

Now, picture the future you. The you who has gone on to assess the dreams of youth, who can appreciate and celebrate that real life turned out differently. And you who unashamedly distilled what was truly important to go after to live a life that included joy, contentment, and even an improbable goal here or there, one that had nothing to do with being a wife or partner, a worker, a mom, or daughter. How does it feel to see her?

Write two or three of the goals down. Maybe it's quilting. Writing. A half-marathon. Only you know.

Write with abandon. This is just for you.

Now, think about your life presently. Is it an unavoidable crisis of health or a set of choices you make daily, perhaps a role you've fallen into as the family cheerleader, that's keeping you from taking baby steps toward your aspirations?

What can you give up to create space for you?

3. What's Wrong with You? Trauma-Informed Care

What's wrong with you?

Long before I actually said it out loud, I'd wondered it about my teenagers. They were acting out. Skipping classes. Drinking. Using recreational drugs. And when I told my youngest daughter, then fifteen, that if she wanted to live in my house, she'd have to follow my rules, she moved out.

I'd spent so much of their teen years making accusations. Trying to regain control. Feeling that their behaviors were a personal attack on me and my parenting.

How could my daughters be so ungrateful? This is what I thought as they exhibited normal, along with a few abnormal teenaged behaviors. Hadn't they seen all I'd done for them?

While I was caught up in being a victim and weaponizing my martyrdom, they were still attending high school, making good grades, and working part-time on the side and participating in sports.

But I saw none of that.

I was so certain that all of our earlier blows were put to bed. The domestic violence impact, the poverty, the kidnapping fallout?

Done. They were finished with trauma. We'd graduated somehow, and could put it all behind us, now.

Weren't we better than this as a family?

It wasn't until I became a trauma-informed trainer at work and learned more about Adverse Childhood Experiences that I realized I'd based my parenting on old-school standards and outdated research that didn't fit what they'd experienced.

Around the same time, when I was new to my role as a juvenile probation supervisor, I was tasked by our then-director to check our program's effectiveness. "Go to the halfway houses, the jails, and correctional facilities where some of our former probationers are, and ask them what we could have done better, and what we did well when they were kids."

There was no presumption of efficacy in this plan. This would not turn into trusted research. Just an information-gathering exercise. Yet I liked the idea of asking the people who had nothing to lose or gain how we could do better for the next generation's delinquent youth. I set out with questionnaires and a list of where these young adults were.

First, let me explain, these were not the juveniles who'd simply made a childhood mistake and skimmed through our system. These weren't simply pot-smokers, shoplifters, or kids who'd toilet papered the neighbor's home. These were the kids who at one time received our most serious consequence, staying in what amounted to a prison for juveniles for up to two years or until the age of 20 if they elected to stay longer. Some had murdered. Some had raped. And everything in between. And now they were men in their early twenties to early thirties, given free rein to comment on how just our justice had actually been.

Boy, did I get an earful.

The questions not only asked what we as professionals could have done better in our programming and in our treatment of them back in the day, but what they wish they would have done differently themselves, what they were proud of, and what were lessons learned that they'd carried into adulthood.

I spoke with a young man in jail who said he'd suffered depression after being separated from his family while in the juvenile center. He'd grown up without routine, any real discipline, and suddenly he was forced to make his bed every day, early in the morning.

"The thing is," he said, "I'd never had a bed before. We slept on the couch with blankets. There were too many of us to have beds. So, I was really proud when I finally learned what to do with sheets. But a hair from my head fell on to the white bedspread, and I was docked points...I wanted to kill myself. Staff didn't know what my home life had been like. They didn't know how hard I was trying. They assumed my life had been like theirs."

We all do this, even though we know better. We meet someone. We get to know them personally or professionally. And we evaluate them based on our set of experiences, assuming — consciously or unconsciously—that there is a baseline of norms and expectations that are universal.

I took copious notes as I went inmate to inmate that day. Seeing me, some of the men were transported back to their youth. "I'm so glad you came to visit!" one exclaimed. "You guys are part of my heart. I always wanted to say thank you for being there for me when my family wasn't."

Every single interview provided bits of insight and wisdom. Some one thing staff had said that either motivated or aggravated; some one way that the daily routines had helped heal or hurt them.

One man recounted a conversation that informed all of my future work. He said that he'd been a constant challenge to staff rules when he was new to our facility, acting out, and putting no effort into the program during the first year of his two-year order. He'd worn the staff's last nerve. Finally, one of the officers told him, "I don't care what you do. You can act out all you like. You'll be here, and I'll get paid and go home. Simple."

That got my attention. Not because it was such an awful thing to say to a kid, but because I'd been guilty of saying a version of that myself to a juvenile so that he might give less energy to driving me crazy.

I asked this man now to clarify what that felt like for him, and what he wanted to hear instead.

"Look, I get it. I was a pain in the ass. But I guess I wanted my probation officer to know that hearing I didn't matter to him actually did matter to me. I'd grown up hearing I was nothing. I'd always been shown that I meant nothing. A kid needs to hear, 'I have faith in you. I think you can do more. You can be more. I care that you succeed, and I want to see you do it.'"

His eyes were soft as he spoke. This had exposed a nerve.

I recalled that conversation whenever I saw subsequent clients. His message became my mantra to them. Later, after making amends, to my own daughters, and, when I worked to motivate myself through hard times, I would repeat it back to myself.

So, let me say it to you: No one but you can appreciate what you've been through to reach this point in your life. I have faith in you and your ability to thrive. I know you can do more. You can be more. You have a unique contribution to add to the world around you. I do care that you succeed, and I want to see you do it.

But you need to believe this about you, too. If you don't already, I'd like to suggest that having this belief becomes an important first goal. Know your history, how it may impact your potential, and let's look at your social support to ensure they promote the atmosphere for healing and change.

Dolly Parton once said, "We cannot direct the wind, but we can adjust the sails."

We must define who we are and where we've been to chart what changes we wish to create.

What Happened to You Matters

The messages from the former delinquent youth were later reinforced by a whole new curriculum I later taught to new employees working with at-risk youth: trauma-informed care.

Though the principles had been around for nearly twenty years, they began trending in 2010. In short, trauma-informed care teaches us to ask, *"What happened to you?"* rather than *"What's wrong with you?"*

Sometimes, we don't have the answers due to our families of origin.

If by chance you come from the family of my dreams, including still-married parents, tight connections with all of your siblings, special recipes handed down by your dear grandma, and you're looking forward to meeting up with them all during your very next holiday, how wonderful. I'm jealous. You can skip this next part.

But that's not my family. And, for that matter, that is not most families. Families like mine are rough in spots, with divorces and estrangements, favored children and sibling rivalries. We may deal with addiction and depression, with anxiety and abuse. We may have case workers, probation officers, multiple dad or mom figures, and discover siblings we had never known existed until they showed up on the genealogy website we have just joined. We may have family members on the sex offender registry. And we watch portrayals of the perfect families on television and want to crawl into a hole.

For better or worse, our earliest experiences of home in the first act of life set the stage for how we will perform in others. It is that place where we are meant to be safe. To be protected from the outside world. It is where we learn how to care for ourselves, where we discover how to behave toward others like future partners and coworkers.

Only too often, it is not. When I was a child abuse investigator, I saw children with an array of physical and mental injuries given to them by their parents. Cracked skulls, scarring, bruises in different stages of healing. And ninety-nine percent of the time, if they were younger than ten or eleven, these children wanted more than anything to remain in their parent's care and stay out of foster care.

Years later, often these same children were on my caseload in juvenile probation. They'd been in and out of foster care. Some witnessed their parent's homicide or suicide. Many were abandoned. Those most likely to reach a successful adulthood were able to see their parents realistically. Maybe they acted out for a while, becoming bullies, destroying property, or running away. And who could blame them? Yet the kids who worried me most were those who seemed embarrassed about loving their parent(s). They felt stained by their parents' choices and acted in. Punishing themselves. Anesthetizing with drugs and alcohol. Self-mutilating.

"It's okay to love your family as they are," I wanted to say to the pimply-faced boy squirming uncomfortably in his chair in my office. "No matter what they've done. You can be proud of them simply because they are yours...it's okay not to love them, too. It doesn't make you a monster. It makes you human."

That's what I wanted to say—would have said if it weren't complete overreach by a government employee. If the parent's presence created too much risk for them, loving the parent needn't translate into living with that parent or having contact until that dynamic had changed.

Which is a lesson that I still struggle to embrace. It's been nearly thirty years since I've seen my mother, who is still alive. My father died in 1995. In my youth, I felt crushed by the weight of their decisions. I blamed them for perpetuating a cycle of family violence and sibling alienation, as though they'd set out to make my life hell.

Parents are our best motivators, either because they were so fantastic during our childhood that we want to copy their style, or because they were not. We can choose to replicate the good stuff. We might accidentally repeat the bad stuff. Or we can wise up, and chart a course to learn how to show up in the world with intention.

I didn't set out to make all the same mistakes my parents did, but I didn't know how not to. The disasters I walked into in my youth, like an early marriage to an older man I hardly knew, seemed inevitable, like a setup somehow. The domestic violence, the later child kidnapping was all like a bad television re-run.

When I learned that I could buck my parents' trends, I accepted the challenge. I made incremental progress. And with each success, I became more grateful to my parents for showing me who I didn't want to be. Not out of anger. Not out of spite. Their history inspired me toward new opportunities that they might not have had. For education. For long-term friendships. For emotional and financial stability. There are so many of us who live life without any direction. I had a perfect map drawn for me of what not to do. Making peace with my own choices and dissecting what I learned from my failures helped me to accept my parents fully.

Learning about trauma-informed care, combined with growing older and growing up while making many of my own mistakes, helped. For my parents' actions to be intentional, it would have required forethought. And there was none of that.

Writing about my own life, I began to wonder about my parents' earlier lives. What had happened to *them*? How was my dad raised? What were the expectations of young men during the time he was being brought up? How did going to war and an early marriage impact him? And for my mom, who often appeared to hate being a mother, what other choices were really available for an uneducated Southern woman of modest means in the late 1940s? Was she correct in thinking that men and her ability to attract one were her only real currency? Could she have pursued an education and a career of her own? What kind of scrutiny would she have faced if she had pursued her real dreams back then?

And what of my older siblings? As a kid, I felt a profound sense of abandonment simply because they had fled a bad home, either voluntarily or after getting displaced by our mother, never looking back to see if I as the youngest would be alright. Like all youngsters, I was developmentally ego-centric, believing everything around me was either caused by or related to me somehow.

Later, I knew better. Each one of them was a mighty phoenix. They had been dished their own portions of hardship and then did whatever was necessary to save themselves. They instinctively knew they had to put on their oxygen mask first and get to a place of strength before they could take on another sibling's needs. And really, it was never their job to be my parent.

Asking *What happened to you?* rather than *What's wrong with you?* that trauma-informed decision- making requires, even with our own families, is freeing. Rooted in empathy and the wisdom that acknowledges that most of us do not set out to hurt or disappoint others, it provides a framework of understanding. It depersonalizes the prior emotional wounds accumulated without green-lighting future bad acts. The things that happened weren't anything to do with you when you were little.

Trauma-informed Care is NOT an Excuse

To be perfectly clear, trauma-informed care does not excuse bad behavior.

When I worked with abuse victims, I co-facilitated a group that went over the many reasons given by their partners for the violence they perpetrated.

Excuses like:

It was the alcohol...
My bad childhood...
I was a Vietnam vet...
My intense love for you made me do it...
I blacked out and don't remember what I did...
It's not me...
It's my mental health.

Women who'd previously sat in silence through other groups became animated in this one. They loved to talk about their partners, sort out their partner's problems, and try to diagnose the problem that was to blame for the abuse. I'd done the same thing myself years before in my marriage. If my husband told me it was job stress that made him cruel, I would work tirelessly to help him find better employment. If he said it was how I looked or kept house, I reinvented myself to be aligned with what he wanted. Anything to keep the relationship together while making the abuse end. So, I understood the women in the group and their laser focus on their partner's needs. They didn't want their partners to get in trouble, didn't want to consider that the problem might be linked to a need of the partner to have power and control.

After creating the long list of reasons women were told led to their abuse, the group facilitator summed it up with a simple question:

"Now that you've looked at why your partner says he abuses, let's ask the important one: What does it matter? What does his reason matter?"

If you are being abused, your abuser's early childhood problems or later-life tragedies are no excuse. You deserve to be treated well. It is not your job to fix anyone else's problems but yours. You did not sign up for a project, but a partner. Leave the fixing for the abuser and the professional support he or she should be seeking, and never harbor guilt for moving on.

But it goes beyond intimate partner relationships. A painful past doesn't give me or you the right to erupt on others, and it's a quick route to thinning our support system. While we'll talk about this more later in a couple of sections, it's worth mentioning now.

Some of us will happily afford our loved ones a free pass that we'd never grant ourselves due to their awful backstory. Others of us, consciously or subconsciously, frame our behavior in the best possible light, filtering out negative things we've said or done or excusing them.

It's likely a coping mechanism. But does it help us move forward? No. It keeps us stuck, and in a victim mindset.

Resources

Trauma-Informed Care: What it Is and Why It's Important by Monique Tello, MD https://www.health.harvard.edu/

When Love Goes Wrong: What to Do When You Can't Do Anything Right by Ann Jones and Susan Schecter

Reflection

What is the difference between blame and accountability?

Is there someone in your life that you've given lots of freedom to do or say abusive things because they have a history of trauma or problems you feel bad about? How do you think that has helped them to heal and to grow?

During challenging times, do you find yourself making excuses to the people in your life as to the reason for your outbursts?

If yes, what will you do differently?

If no, to what do you attribute your success?

4: Your Inheritance

By the time my oldest sister Wanda received the news that she had cancer, it was deemed incurable. She was only in her sixties. Wanda was the first female skipper of a commercial fishing vessel I've known. A former carpenter. A single mom, who at fifteen was discarded like trash by our mom into an area of Anchorage, Alaska where sex workers congregated. Now, she was fading away.

We siblings were part of a group text, keeping her company from our respective homes around the country. And it was here where Wanda finally began releasing childhood memories, one by one. Perfectly preserved, yet calcified and heavy like a stone baby, those memories had not faded with time. They pressed down hard until they could find their way out.

I remember a conversation a decade earlier with Wanda when she was incredulous that anyone would go to counseling to address the things that went on in our home as children. "Why would you want to relive it?"

I'd never want you (or her) to get stuck reliving hard things for no reason. We do it because when we try to gloss over old scars like my sister had, they don't heal. They're left merely lying in wait.

"But I'm mentally strong," women of our generation sometimes indicate. "I just got through it on my own. I can do it again."

Maybe. You can release trauma several other ways besides counseling. But the point is, it must be released. Unpacked. Processed. Addressed. Or they weigh us down. Make us heavy in so many ways. Even shorten our lives.

It was the Adverse Childhood Experiences Study (ACEs), one of the largest investigations of neglect and childhood abuse and later-life outcomes of health and well-being, which confirmed this. It's not an inevitability, a death sentence, or an unmovable fact. But it's solid science that's identified serious risk factors.

What I'm asking of you is to assess your inheritance, the legacy left to you by your family experience. You don't have to decide whether your parents or childhood were good or bad. I'm asking you to take a look back with objectivity and see how things that happened a long time ago are impacting you now.

Think of it as an estate sale. When a family member dies, you may need to hire a neutral party to assess their leftover belongings before deciding whether to keep or offload them. Now that you are years removed from your childhood, you get to be the neutral assessor.

What are the questions covered in ACEs?

The ACEs study goes over what happened to you, around you, or what didn't happen that should have in the form of childhood neglect. From witnessing domestic violence as a child, having a parent incarcerated, a parent who experienced mental health problems and beyond, there are ten different questions asked in the original ACE's quiz. Issues like racism and poverty are also included in a more recent version. This long-term study, done on 17,000 middle- aged white people who belonged to HMOs, gave cause-and-effect proof that the emotional wounds that fester inside us destroy our health.

Let's do a little self-inventory to see if we have any emotional hotspots left over from our childhoods and take the

GROUNDED IN GRIT: TURN YOUR CHALLENGES INTO SUPERPOWERS

ACE's test online at CDC.org. (ACEs quiz alone on a page with references to the CDC.)

Why, you ask?

Well, one, knowing the weight of your emotional baggage enhances self-awareness. And two, the beliefs we hold about ourselves and the world around us are often influenced by ACEs without us even realizing it. The things that happened to us as children, good or bad, can have a huge impact on how we respond to our world. And the science behind the ACEs study is irrefutable. There is a direct, cause-and-effect relationship between how many toxic traumas one experiences in youth, and in (for just one example) how much cortisol flows through their veins, creating overproduction of glucose and increasing blood sugar levels which can contribute to problems like obesity, high blood pressure, and decreased moods.

I'm writing this in 2021 through 2023, the fourth year in a row that life expectancy in the United States has declined. The increased death rate of middle- aged people from all types of socioeconomic backgrounds and ethnicities is largely due to obesity, opioids, liver disease, and suicides.

More than half of us have an ACE score. And ACE scores of 6 or more increase the likelihood of early death by two decades if they remain unaddressed. Two decades.

If your ACE score is high, but you don't have the associated mental, physical, or behavioral health problems including obesity or substance abuse, fantastic! Can you identify some of the supports, mentors, and other buffers that have helped you become the resilient person you are?

If you have associated dysfunction with your ACE score, like paralyzing anxiety, depression, substance abuse, or health concerns, are you willing to address them with professional help?

Unaddressed traumas create handicaps. They spark unwarranted fight-or-flight reactions during ordinary conflicts. They can hobble our ability to accurately read the emotions of others, which creates all kinds of problems, at home, at work, in life.

Knowing your ACE score gives insight into your stress response. It's like weighing your carry-on baggage before you get on a plane. You'll reduce the element of surprise.

Don't Forget the good stuff that happened, too!

I released the emotional heaviness from my youth when I figured out that my family dysfunction was neither unique, personal, or intentional. It was an inheritance that I could accept and deed to the next generation, or that I could reject. The shame I'd concealed. The devastation and rage about violence and desertion. They were valid feelings based on my perception of some harsh realities. I had choices about how to deal with those feelings, and who I would trust to remain in the emotionally and physically safe environment I committed to living in.

Annabelle "Bee" Baumann's career as an author and stand-up comedian is rooted in her experience growing up in a stable foster home from infancy to age 12, and her eventual uprooting by her mother to bring Bee home to live in poverty and instability with seven other siblings. Now living in Germany, Bee's humor unpacks memories previously painful and shameful. A Black woman, she's taken her childhood experiences of not belonging and parlayed it into a career today helping the largely Caucasian population in Germany as an intercultural business trainer.

"The past is something we can stand on rather than hide from after we've done our healing work...We don't have to lose any of our past, but we include it in our life's tapestry," Bee said.

Accepting our family is critical if we are to accept ourselves. We can take pride in them simply because they are ours. We can choose to accept our family, to love them even if it defies logic. Yet if they jeopardize our emotional or physical safety and refuse any interventions to address it, we can choose unapologetically to love them, or not love them, from a distance. We can cease contact until the dynamic changes, or permanently cease contact if it does not. Carefully selecting whom we allow to have access to our time and energy, even if we are related to them, is an important step in creating space and energy for the changes you are committed to making in your life.

We spend plenty of time going over what's gone wrong and how it's affected us. What happened to us before birth and in our early years matters. But not just the bad stuff. Let's consider those people that during our lifetime have shown up, expectedly or unexpectedly, and made a difference by opening their hearts and providing support. From schoolteachers to kind neighbors, coaches, and clergy, if we experienced adverse childhood experiences, yet intersected with good doses of positive childhood experiences, our risk for depression and poor mental health decreases commensurately.

In a study published in the Journal of American Medical Association Pediatrics in November of 2019, Dr. Christina Bethell defined seven positive childhood experiences (PCEs) that could reduce the long-term impact of ACEs. Like whether the participant reported that as a child, they could talk to their family about their feelings, and their family stood by them during hard times. If they had a sense of belonging in high school. Were they supported by friends, and have two non-parents who took genuine interest in them? Were they safe and protected by an adult in their home?

The more positive childhood experiences they had, the less likely their Adverse Childhood Experiences would cause poor mental health later.

Years ago, I wrote my memoir, choosing to tell the story of part of my life in the present tense, as though it were all happening just now to make the writing more compelling. But writing it in present tense made it impossible for the older, wiser me to comment on what I know now, or to speculate on things I learned from research. When I did promotional events, I was often asked how I'd emerged from some of my family's brokenness. Birth order had been on my side, I told them, realizing that my siblings had to be the answer.

I don't remember some of the things my older siblings did for me but heard consistently how they read to me as a baby, taught me to read and write early, and cared for me to help our mother. As the years passed, one sister, just five years older than me, worried that I would get hurt while she was at school activities or on dates, so she let me tag along. The other siblings I grew up with would have helped, but they'd already been extricated from our home and were fending for themselves as best they could. Then, when my mom moved away, leaving me, the only child left in the home at 13, it was this sister who let me move with her to another state.

GROUNDED IN GRIT: TURN YOUR CHALLENGES INTO SUPERPOWERS

Let me be clear: I do not have many fond memories of this time in my life. Everything felt uncertain. Would we have a home? Would I ever make friends at this new school? Would we eat, and when?

Yet I knew that I had a sister who was trying to help me and had other family who would have if they could, had friends back in Alaska who were cheering for me, and had educators and counselors at my new school who saw my abilities. I also remember the upstairs neighbors in our apartment building. Two Japanese exchange students attending college named Tippy and Takko, beautiful and bright women in their early twenties, invited me, a fuzzy-haired, chubby girl with thick glasses, over sometimes while my sister waited tables at night. How special I felt to be invited into the world of makeup and textbooks and stories of their home, a place I could only imagine.

All of these buffers built on one another.

In her book *The Thank You Project: Cultivating Happiness One Letter at a Time,* author Nancy Davis Kho told the story of how she wrote fifty thank you cards to fifty people who'd influenced her life over the past five decades. The experience not only increased her happiness but helped facilitate the process of teaching her brain to seek out gratitude.

Don't be afraid to take an unflinching look at your roots. To acknowledge how your early family and life experiences help shape who you are and how you show up in your world, and to celebrate the tapestry that's led you to today.

Resources

Acesstudy.org

US Life Expectancy Dropped Third Year in a Row medicaleconomics.com/

Persistence U Podcast with Lizbeth, episode 56: Annabelle "Bee" Baumann on What Happens When a Stranger Shows Up at the Home You've Always Known the First 12 Years of Life to Take you Away?

Gurrrl, You Ain't Crazy: Self-Help for the Funny Bone by Annabelle "Bee" Baumann

Study on Seven Positive Childhood Experiences https://www.ncbi.nlm.nih.gov/pmc/articles/PMC6735495/

The Thank You Project: Cultivating Happiness One Letter at a Time by Nancy Davis Kho

Reflection

Think about a particularly rough time in your own life. Who (or what) were the buffers? What positive experiences did they provide you with?

Write a thank you letter to one of them, even if they're no longer living, or if you can't find the person to give the letter to. Let that person know what their impact was on you.

Imagine that you have an opportunity to be a buffer. What will you do to make a difference?

5. Thinking Errors Balanced With Self-Compassion

"You're such a klutz!" I told myself as the glass in my hand slipped through my fingers and shattered, leaving pieces large and small all over the floor. I'd been out of my volatile relationship with my husband for months by now, but I didn't need him to treat me badly any longer. I did a pretty terrific job of it myself.

What happens when we punish ourselves with cruel thoughts and words?

We're much more likely to struggle with either depression or perfectionism.

When we mentally beat ourselves up, we risk receiving constructive criticism- valuable feedback that might help us grow- from a boss, a partner, or a total stranger we have requested assistance from, as fighting words. What we say to ourselves, whether by thoughts or actual words, has everything to do with how we communicate with others. The internal dialogue that we've developed up until now can get in the way of productive communication if it remains unchecked.

I wonder now what lessons I would have remembered from my shelter stay and ongoing support services had I not gone to work at the same agency years later. Because when I became one of the group facilitators, I memorized that curriculum on setting boundaries, communication styles, and conflict resolution that I'd previously breezed through, as if my life depended on it. And eventually, it did.

GROUNDED IN GRIT: TURN YOUR CHALLENGES INTO SUPERPOWERS

My commitment to change had become strong enough that I no longer thought to myself, "I hope I can do this," but rather, "I'll do what it takes. I'll just have to learn how."

Back then, I thought of it as wanting to take care of myself as I did for my daughters. A good parent concerns themselves with how their child is fed, when they sleep, their safety, and later, the child's educational goals, and with whom their child keeps company. They want the best for their child. I needed to want the best for me, to do the best for me. Because didn't I deserve that as much as anyone else?

Many years later, Dr. Kristin Neff gave this concept a term now embraced by the research community: *self-compassion.*

Self-compassion is granting the same empathy and concern to yourself that you give to others who are suffering. It means acknowledging your suffering and your humanity. It means that you work toward change out of the belief that you deserve more, not due to shame and self-loathing.

According to Dr. Neff, the three components involve being kind to oneself, accepting our human imperfections, and accepting that each of us will go through hard times rather than buying into the belief that life has it in for us somehow.

It does not mean you will be overly indulgent. Filled with self-pity. Destined to live a wimpy life. It simply means that you notice your pain and self-soothe.

"Speak to yourself with love, kindness, and praise—remind yourself frequently that you are loved, special, worthy, divine, and capable...The tone and kindness with which we speak to ourselves and others creates our environments," offers author Thomas Blackwell in his book, *The Liberty of Our Language Revealed.*

My daughters were tiny when I first saw comedian Al Franken's portrayal of affirmation guru Stuart Smalley on Saturday Night Live. Smalley was a tenderhearted character embracing recovery who looked into a mirror and said, "I'm good enough, I'm smart enough, and, doggone it, people like me."

I couldn't wait to teach the girls, especially my two-year-old, who inexplicably spoke with a Jersey accent, to say it. It took a bit of coaxing, but as she repeated the words back to me over and over, my mood lifted. Energy-producing affirmations to a woman fresh out of a violent marriage. *I'm good enough. I'm smart enough. And, doggone it, people like me.*

The word *enough* was an important piece of the message. Realistic. Not an impossibility. It wasn't about pretending I was Mother Teresa or Albert Einstein. But I was good enough. Smart enough. And some people did like me well enough.

Effective positive self-talk is not rooted in aspiration but in acceptance, compassion, and reality. Had I repeated "I am perfect!" twenty times a day, it would have meant nothing. For me, reworking my inner dialogue was to remind me that I was human, with strengths and weaknesses, no more or no less worthy of safety, of the stable environment I'd always craved, and which I was determined to carve out for my little girls, worthy of significance. The messages were a fusion of affirmation and accountability that helped nudge me toward the life I wanted. Positive self-talk guided by self-compassion, filtered for thinking errors, creates a combination that inspires transformation.

I can't believe I did that! becomes *I'm only human. I'm still a work in progress.*

I should be farther along in my life becomes *I will do the work to make progress on my own time scale.*

I'm not strong enough of a person to make it through this awful period in my life becomes *I've never been challenged in this way before, yet I'm capable of doing hard things and look forward to gaining new emotional muscle.*

I'm so miserable that I deserve to buy these expensive boots becomes *It's normal that I feel awful under the circumstances. But won't it be great to get through this time while paying off debt?*

I can't leave this toxic relationship becomes *It's okay to love someone who's not good for me or to me, but that doesn't mean I will stay with anyone who treats me poorly.*

I hate exercise, becomes *I can commit to walking a few minutes a day and building on that over time since I understand it helps me fight depression and manage my anxieties. I know I don't have to like it.*

I'm tired of asking for help. I just want to be in control of my own life becomes *I could really benefit from the additional support being offered and will give this a chance.*

It would be too much for me to talk to someone and relive the trauma I've just been through when I'm only now starting to feel better becomes *I deserve to invest time in my healing so that I increase the odds of being able to move forward.*

It's important that you show yourself both love and kindness. But that doesn't mean it's time to go easy on yourself. You *are* capable of doing hard things, like facing your own faulty thinking. Like asking for help. Like being uncomfortable as you change old patterns. You can choose to do what is good for you, reminding yourself that you are worthy of being treated well, by you and those you allow to share space with you. And if you want your future to be remarkably different from your past, you absolutely must.

Self-Compassion Does Not Equal Self-Justification

Self-compassion is essential for forgiving yourself when you make mistakes and for getting out of your own way, but it's not meant to be used as a get-out-of-jail-free card. Nor is it designed to lead you into self-defeating choices or to allow you to excuse your bad behavior. If you're reframing self-talk as a way to shirk responsibility . . . well, just imagine me standing there waving a giant red flag. I'm all too familiar with this particular mind game.

"What's that, Mom?," my daughter asked when she was eight after spotting the fluorescent tag dangling from our front door. We'd just arrived home after shopping to find a shut-off notice from the electric company. Again.

Sometimes we ran out of money because I was the sole supporter of two kids. But other times, it was because I let my self-talk go rogue, mollifying myself before making a bad choice. "*You deserve that dinner out,*" or *You're already so deep in debt. How could another small purchase possibly hurt?* All while avoiding paying my obligations.

Soon, my graduate school internship with adult felons would teach me to correct my thinking when I co-facilitated groups on thinking errors, originally called criminal thinking errors by clinicians Yochelson and Samenow in the 70s. The psych world calls them cognitive distortions. Often subconscious, they're unrealistic or inaccurate ways of thinking, according to therapist and writer Amy Morin, who wrote about them in Psychology Today's blog on what mentally strong people don't do. While Stanton and Samenow identified fifty originally, Morin lists ten common thought distortions. They're worth looking at, so I've included a link in the resources where you can learn more. Left unchallenged, thinking errors help us justify to ourselves why we are victims of circumstance, why the world is picking on us, why we can't possibly be expected to move forward. Here are some oldies but goodies:

Emotional reasoning: When irrational thoughts are twisted to seem rational. I applied this with gusto to my budget problems. For example, I'd tell myself once I was so far in the financial hole, I might as well spend on some other discretionary item rather than pay what I owed.

Minimizing: A sixty-year-old offender refused to take responsibility for pushing his diminutive wife down the stairs, letting the judge know he'd never actually abused her. "I never hit her, I just pushed her, and didn't know she was so close to the stairs. Besides, she bruises easily."

Fortune-telling: A young man on my probation caseload was nearing adulthood without any parents to help him make the transition. To my chagrin, he refused to get help from his tribe as he made his way back from addiction, despite the fact that they offered services and resources if he demonstrated his seriousness to remain sober. "They'll just ask me to do a whole bunch of things that have nothing to do with getting me to my goal, just like other agencies have in the past. I don't need them." Rather than giving it a try to let the future unfold, he cut off his options to avoid risk.

Victim stance: A middle-aged woman sat in the abuse recovery group. The topic was looking for red flags in an abusive relationship. "You can't help who you're attracted to," she shrugged. "You love who you love. I guess these are just the cards I've been dealt."

Thinking Better

Let's pay attention to the thoughts swirling around in our head because thoughts guide our feelings, which guide our actions. And we need our actions to help us establish bullet-proof habits of self-care.

The right thoughts will keep us accountable and moving forward. The wrong ones will keep us feeling weak.

I found I couldn't do better until I learned to think better. I stopped letting faulty thinking gain traction. Once I did, I could slowly rise out of problems like crushing debt, inflated expectations of friends or my kids. I could stop squashing my own goals and dreams before I'd given myself the chance to try them on.

Too often, our thinking errors hold us back. They transmit subconscious notions that we can't do any better. That we're a victim. And being a victim reinforces a sense of powerlessness. It ignores our inner strength. Our potential. Our ability to flourish. These thinking errors leave no room for change.

Now, just identifying thinking errors as they randomly appear can be incredibly helpful. You may find that you have a negative, self-defeating commentary running through your head day and night, and there's no time like the present to face it with compassion. (See Reflection section below.) It's also helpful to focus the lens, particularly when it comes to your hopes and dreams and how you get in your own way in achieving them. For example:

Dream: I've always wanted to travel the globe.

Negative self-talk: But I'm single, on a slim budget, get lost A LOT. (Can you tell this one's mine?)

Thinking error: These details must be perfectly aligned in order for me to green-light my dreams.

Self-compassion: I'm not perfect, but my ability to manage my quirks stateside won't disappear once I use my passport and hop continents. And my experiences steering through awful times tell me I can do it again if I run into trouble.

Things that I learned about me that make my dreams probable: I persist through difficulties and can adapt and create support networks wherever I go. I can be comfortable being uncomfortable. Clumsiness, ignorance, financial resource deficits are no match for persistence. Instead of lingering in *I can't*, I've trained myself to reconfigure until I can say, *I'm not yet sure how I will.* Not always right away. Not seamlessly. Not without bouts of self-doubt. But eventually. And then I go about finding a way.

And I know you can, too.

Resources

Ten Thinking Errors That Will Crush You by Amy Morin

Inside the Criminal Mind by Dr. Stanton E Samenow

Reflection

What negative messages are you telling yourself that keep you from reaching your dreams? Are you falling into the trap of thinking that your dreams should fall at the bottom of your priority list?

Can you identify thinking errors worth tossing out? And if you implement self-compassion and address your thinking errors, what do you come up with?

Do you ever tune in to the thoughts and judgments you have about yourself? Do they set you up for success?

What messages are in your mind when you make a misstep? Could you imagine saying them to a cherished friend of yours who'd made the same mistake?

Let's put it all together. Fill the following out (and use it as a template again and again when needed!):

Dream:

Negative self-talk:

Thinking error:

Self-compassion:

Things that I learned about me that make my dreams probable:

Part II: Strong Communication

6. Communication Equation

"So, what happened when you talked to him about it?" I asked my coworker, a fellow probation supervisor now talking about a rogue employee who'd yet again missed a critical deadline with the court.

"Well," she said, looking down, shifting in her chair, "I haven't talked to him yet. He's about to go on vacation with his family, and I didn't want to bring it up and ruin his trip."

On its surface, this may appear to be an act of kindness. But this kind of passivity, this indirect communication in which it's seemingly all right to talk about a person's conduct to others while not addressing the actual person in question, is anything but.

"I'm just venting," is the typical response. But if that venting isn't followed by action toward resolution, it's character assassination at worst, and ineffective communication at best.

This communication style was rampant in my twenty years spent working in juvenile probation. Once, I spoke to my direct supervisor and requested that our entire staff receive no-cost training on healthy communication in the workplace.

In a profession like probation work predicated on personal accountability and the capacity to influence the behavior of another, when it came to how we employees spoke to each other, we'd mastered the art of mousiness.

For a minute, it seemed promising. And then came the response.

"It wouldn't change anything, and people wouldn't like it."

People "liking it" was never the goal. Having agreed upon expectations for conflict resolution, giving staff the tools needed to have tough conversations, was.

I know for sure that I hadn't liked it. I'd learned first as a client, then as an employee at Abused Women's Aid in Crisis, that assertive communication was expected. I tested that out by gossiping about a board member once and got my fanny handed to me on a silver platter by my supervisor. My passive with intermittent aggressive communication style would not be tolerated, and it required I learn a skill set completely foreign to me. Cue the mandatory training!

In my house growing up, we kids had witnessed periods of normalcy, long enough to relax our collective shoulders. So, when the screaming, the slamming of doors, the injury of a sibling occurred, we learned to fear both conflict and anger.

That, and the fact that women in my generation were raised to be pleasing and sweet, and behavior to the contrary often resulted in a label to be avoided. That still holds true today. I worked with a woman in her twenties recently who told me she quit a job she desperately needed to keep because she didn't know how to set limits with a coworker. The coworker first requested, then later demanded, rides to and from work, running errands in between. My coworker could barely pay her bills with the job, but saying no to requests was too foreign to her, so she took the financial hit.

Ugh!

For years, I'd tried to keep my own anger bridled, trying to keep an emotional Spanx on, but bits of repressed fury made their way out at unexpected times. It scared me. *I* scared me.

GROUNDED IN GRIT: TURN YOUR CHALLENGES INTO SUPERPOWERS

We've all come from different family, cultural, and generational backgrounds. Some of us are managing old wounds. We have a different frame of reference for how communication should be done. And as someone who's worked inside, in collaboration with and against government agencies throughout my time as a crime victim and later as a public servant, strong communication is the personal flotation device needed once life ruptures.

Gender Roles: Raised on the Message that Men Are Leaders, Women, Pleasers

"You want me to go *where?*" I asked, feeling the color draining from my 28-year-old face as my new boss told me that I would be attending a weekend conference for lesbian and gay adults.

I was straight. It was the early 90s, and I was certain hers was a terrible idea. "Won't they think I'm spying on them?" I asked her. In truth, I was more concerned about my own discomfort about all things sexual rather than whether gay and lesbian strangers would think I was a secret shopper.

The older me looks back on this with great amusement. Not the fact that I couldn't find my voice and admit to my own ignorance, but that I believed this conference would be about sex.

It was not. I can't remember what the theme was, but I do remember what I learned at one particular workshop about historical gender roles and their impact on four basic communication styles.

Men were considered leaders if they spoke their mind. They were strong. Powerful. The go-to guy. They knew how to set boundaries.

Yet women had long been discouraged from advocating for their own needs, lest they be perceived as too masculine, too bitchy. We'd been trained by our moms and women from prior generations to hint at what we wanted. To be pleasers. To withhold affection and retain bitterness, since we weren't permitted to say what we thought. We learned to be **passive**, assuming the needs of others were more important than our own. And passive communication comes with its own rewards, like avoiding or putting off conflict, being well-liked, and not getting blamed for anything.

Passive's close relative was **passive aggression**, where the communicator made fleeting efforts to express their feelings, perhaps using sarcasm, giving the silent treatment, or carrying messages to and from others. It's being angry in secret. Always indirectly. "I don't know if you realized that X is mad at you right now and I thought you should know." Or "I wish I had time to get an education like you are, but my husband won't help with the kids," (having never asked her husband.). Passive-aggressive communication may involve gossip. Rather than telling the person who has aggrieved you, you tell everyone else. "I don't want to hurt their feelings," you reason. Psychologist Dr. Nick Wignall defines passive-aggressive communication as being when "you're too angry to keep quiet and too afraid to be honest."

Aggressive communicators prioritize themselves. They communicate at the expense of others to get their own mission achieved, and seem to maintain control over their circumstances, themselves, and people around them. The aggressive person believes that only their rights matter, and that respecting opinions and rights of others is a sign of

GROUNDED IN GRIT: TURN YOUR CHALLENGES INTO SUPERPOWERS

weakness. The consequence of aggressive communication is having a limited support system due to alienating others, and a stress reaction when things don't go as the aggressive communicator desires.

The skill worth mastering is **assertive communication**. Assertive communicators take responsibility for their thoughts and feelings. They courageously engage in conflict when it's necessary. They have difficult conversations directly. They look for a win-win solution whenever possible and reduce their stress level because their relationships are based on trust and authenticity.

Being assertive can aid with self-confidence. It can earn respect. It creates possibilities where people with differing views or who are in conflict can each emerge as winners. And it presumes that the relationship is valuable enough to invest in and that each person's perspective is important.

Let's return to four types of communication and look at examples of them in action.

Your adult daughter has gone through a personal crisis and wants to move home. You've just gotten used to your empty nest, and like having the extra time for yourself without the cleaning and cooking you'd previously done. You want to help, but there's an uncomfortable conversation to be had:

1. **Passive**: You tell yourself *I'm sure she's going through a hard time and knows this is only temporary. It'll be great to spend extra time together. I don't need to pile on my expectations.*
2. **Passive-aggressive**: You run into your daughter's closest friend at the store, who tells you how relieved

your daughter will be to have a place to return to. You say, "Yep, just as I was getting the hang of living alone and having a neat house, she's back," knowing that her friend will relay the message to her.
3. **Aggressive:** After no conversation about boundaries or expectations, you affix a contract for your daughter to sign to her bedroom door that details a list of rules you expect her to abide by.
4. **Assertive:** You ask your daughter if the two of you could meet for coffee before the move-in to talk about how to make a smooth transition and get a feel for what each person needs to make the arrangement a success.

Being assertive doesn't guarantee good outcomes, but it does produce goodwill. It allows you to unpack your feelings as they arise, to advocate for yourself while not alienating others.

On the communication continuum, I'd begun as passive. I operated from a silent belief that the wishes of others were more important than my own. Society and organized religion confirmed it. A woman was to be submissive to the man she loved. He knew best. She should trust that.

But that wasn't true. My husband didn't know best. He wanted control of me and didn't act in my best interest. I played along, but my anger festered. And then I shifted toward passive- aggressive communication. Trying to please him, then alternately giving him the silent treatment. I once destroyed objects he loved in a fit of anger. I savored my hurt feelings and collected slights. I shifted between being a doormat to wanting to burn the house down, then returning to doormat status again.

When I left my husband, all that anger that had yet to be expressed was still roiling inside me. It took a long time for me to learn how to properly express my emotions and manage my anger. But to grow and maintain a support system, to learn to accept and like myself, to succeed in many of my goals, it was an important skill to master, and merits more attention in the next chapter.

Resources

Assertiveness and the 4 Communication Styles by Dr. Nick Wignall

Reflection

What kind of communication style do you use primarily?

What was the communication style modeled in the home by your parents?

Upon reflection, how do you think the expectations of how women should behave have influenced your communication style?

7. Assertive Communication Fundamentals

"Do you mind not posting this on social media?," a friend of mine asked once after we took a picture together. And before I could ask why, she explained, "I was supposed to be having dinner with my sister. I didn't want to go, though."

And just like that, the fun time we'd had was forgotten. I was left to wonder how many times when I'd asked her to get together that she found it necessary to create an excuse instead of saying no.

I could hardly blame her though. I was no better. My martyr-style solution meant that I would have gone through with the dinner and then resented my sister for it.

As women, we're told it's rude to be direct. It's aggressive to be blunt. And who wants to be aggressive?

I was watching daytime TV recently when actor Elizabeth Olsen mentioned how her sisters taught her that No is a full sentence.

Example: Your friend texts to ask if you'd like to have lunch. You're beat. Or broke. Or not hungry.

Bottom line: Now's not a good time.

You could say you're exhausted. Or don't have funds. Or that you're full. Or you could say, "No. Thank you."

Can you imagine?

Just no.

So freeing.

But what if you don't feel comfortable with a simple no just yet? Your neighbor calls and invites you to an event. You had looked forward all week to having a quiet night in your slippers with a good book. Say, "No thank you. I already have plans." Because you do. No one but you need to know what they are. And the last person you want to flake out on is you.

No guilt.

No apology.

No explanation.

Just **no**.

It helps to practice no in these low-stakes examples, because when times are tough, and you're called upon by a lawyer or a former partner or a boss, you don't want to answer off the cuff.

Hint: Practice saying, "Thank you. Please let me get back to you."

And then do it. Get back to them after you've had a moment or a day (at most) to sort your thoughts.

If you're a recovering martyr like me, you may feel the need to say Yes to requests for a favor, as an example, worrying, *If not me, who'll help? Who will do the thing I've been asked to accomplish?*

But is that your problem to solve? Saying yes to something you don't want to do not only frustrates you, but it deprives another person of the opportunity to step up.

My friend Margot told me about a friend of hers who prefaces her own asks—like "Can you give my daughter a ride to school?" with "Don't say yes unless this request has your name on it."

How perfect is that? A gentle reminder attached to her request that reduces feelings of obligation.

But we don't need thoughtful friends like my friend Margot has. We can offer this wise advice to ourselves. We can mentally nudge ourselves to say, "Let me get back to you," and take a breather before we say no or yes. Make that your reflex if saying no feels too foreign to you. You'll feel more in control of your responses, more authentic in your relationships, and more in charge of your time and life.

Boundaries First

For us recovering martyrs, let's talk about boundaries for a moment.

What *are* boundaries?

When I co-facilitated groups for abused women, we called boundaries an imaginary fence that protects your heart and your body. Boundaries keep us safe. We teach small kids to set boundaries when we tell them about "Good touch-bad touch." Remember that? The lesson we empower little ones with about not allowing anyone to touch them in certain areas of their body, and to tell a safe adult if that happens prevent abuse.

But what about us adults? Do we get any training on how and when to get out of an untenable situation? Whether we're being insulted, intimidated, isolated, or threatened, we too should feel empowered to say no, or set limits without the fear of reprisals. Even when an innocuous request is made by a genuinely nice person that goes against our abilities or values or bandwidth, we can set boundaries. Setting limits with others is a true act of self-care. Like a list of user instructions, setting limits is conditioned on the belief that we matter.

There are many reasons to set boundaries. To maintain safety. To express your personal preferences, beliefs, and priorities. If there is something that evokes feelings of emotional or physical unrest and you're aware of it, healthy relationships should allow room for this to be communicated by you.

For instance, if you're someone who's loved to be a listening ear to your friends and family in crisis, only to find that you've inadvertently become an unpaid 9-1-1 operator who is throwing herself into problems not her own, you may need to set a boundary around your time.

"I've loved being part of your support system and will continue to support you. But I need to take care of me, too. I'm asking you to diversify your support system and not call me more than once a week, and no longer call past 8 pm on weeknights. Let's talk about who else you can look to for support."

Personally, I get a feeling of apprehension that I can't shake if someone stops by my house unannounced. I loathe surprises. That doesn't mean the person stopping by did anything wrong. So, I set a boundary, telling my friends not to drop by unannounced. Then I painted a sign and affixed it to my door reinforcing the message for neighbors and politicians. A home-made boundary.

Setting boundaries is essential to good communication. When you let others know the guidelines you have for yourself, you're allowing them to connect with you without stumbling on something sensitive, or behaving in a way that you find unpleasant or unacceptable.

.

Say What You Mean So That Others Will Hear You

Okay, so we've learned about boundaries and that "No" is indeed a complete sentence. So, what are the assertive communication fundamentals?

That you commit to expressing yourself in a respectful yet direct way to make your point known. Not to be right. Not to make the other party feel bad. Not to "win." That you find a good time for the other person to talk if you can't be assertive in the moment, but that you also not allow the window of time to close by waiting too long. That you listen more than you talk. That you make eye contact, try to keep your voice level, and use statements that describe your own feeling about the behavior or circumstance, and how it impacts you.

There are a lot of "I" statements needed in assertive communication, because you're taking responsibility for your own feelings. No one can make you feel any certain way. You always have a choice as to how you react and reply. This message was one that I first heard and later taught at the abused women's crisis center which encapsulated the definition of empowerment. Even when people say or do unthinkable things, you are in charge of you. Is your self-esteem low after years of adversity? Guess who's the only person responsible for the fix? You.

Nailing this when asking for help is important.

"I feel hopeless when I call your agency and don't get a returned call, week after week. I don't know how to make progress without your input. Can you help me, or tell me who can?"

Or "I feel annoyed when you call me to get together for lunch and spend the entire hour talking about yourself, over and over. It seems like you're using me as an armchair therapist, and that you don't care about me or what's happening in my life."

***

Let's return to the four types of communication and apply them to everyday life when you're not dealing with a friend or family member. Let's say you have a called the Social Security Administration. (This is made up and not based on my real interactions with them.)

You've filed an application for help. The application says to wait ten business days before expecting a confirmation email. Then, follow up.

On day twenty-one, you consider calling.

1. Passive: You tell yourself that surely they're a busy agency. *I won't bother them by calling. I'm sure they're busy.*

2. Passive- aggressive: You post on Facebook, with a link to the agency. "Anyone else have trouble getting a hold of these government asshats? I've been waiting forever and can't get a response."

3. Aggressive: You call and with a raised voice ask if you can speak with a supervisor. "Is there anyone who actually knows what they're doing in your office?"

4. Assertive: "Hi. I filed my application three weeks ago but haven't received the promised confirmation email. I feel like I'm stuck in limbo. Can you please help or direct me on how best to get a hold of the person who can?"

Communicating assertively or in an aggressive fashion can be dangerous when you're dealing with a narcissist or an abusive personality. I would never coach anyone on how to keep the peace in those relationships, nor would I want to pretend that communicating assertively is the key to a good, safe outcome.

I would love to tell you that I only communicate assertively. That emotions never run wild and that I don't ever try to win

GROUNDED IN GRIT: TURN YOUR CHALLENGES INTO SUPERPOWERS

a conflict. That simply isn't true. Like hitting my goal weight, I recognize that maintenance of it means I stay within a five-pound range. The same with communication. Whether it's a deep personality flaw or a remnant of my childhood, I often fight the urge to win. To be right. And to get my point across at the expense of another. The awareness of this deficit means I can recalibrate and self-correct. It may require that I apologize. That I review my thinking errors.

Assertive communication is a skill that you can learn and practice. By managing your thoughts, emotions, and communication style, you'll have the secret sauce for success as you engage others to walk with you during challenging times.

Traci Philips, career coach and author, was a guest on my podcast recently and spoke about dealing with a much anticipated but difficult-from-the-start pregnancy years ago that left her managing a team of specialists who weren't always sensitive to her feelings, or the way awful information was delivered.

Traci knew that remaining in control of her emotions, despite her fluctuating hormones, fear for her child's safety, and her sheer exhaustion around so many unanticipated twists and turns, was critical. She couldn't afford to alienate any part of the team. But when the time came to address how she was being spoken to, and the impact it had on her feelings of well-being, she didn't hold back, using plenty of *I* statements.

"Mrs. Philips," another doctor on the team said to the new mom after hearing the communication, "We all could learn a lot from you. Thank you." The doctor said that it was powerful to hear Traci advocate for herself, and that the medical team would make changes in their practice after receiving her valuable feedback.

Traci said that even now, she asks herself in tough moments what is the message she needs to communicate, how does she want to be received in the world, and does the message need to be addressed now, or is there a better time to do it?

The idea of finding the right time to address a conflict is brilliant, letting emotions settle, respecting those important conversations that need to be had at the right place and time for both parties whenever possible. But let too much time pass, and it's tempting not to address the issue at all. Sometimes that's okay. Things sort themselves. Other times, it becomes just another resentment to collect, another reason you'll subconsciously want to pounce the next time some other issue arises.

Resources

Setting Healthy Boundaries in Your Relationships/ zencenter.org

Persistence U with Lizbeth, episode 17: Traci Philips on When a High Risk Pregnancy Inspired Traci Philips to Learn the Art of Having Courageous Conversations

GROUNDED IN GRIT: TURN YOUR CHALLENGES INTO SUPERPOWERS

Reflection

Think of a request you've begrudgingly and routinely said yes to. It could be a small request, like going to coffee with a pleasant-enough person whose company you simply don't enjoy.

Now, picture you building a fence around you. Visualize you choosing from one of the responses:

I'll need to get back to you."

"I'm afraid I won't be able to this time."

"No, thank you. But I appreciate you asking."

"No."

Which response feels best for you? How does it feel when you imagine saying it?

8: Let's Put Those Skills in Writing: The Key to Holding Service Providers and Government Agencies Accountable

Dear District Attorney Minshull,

I have tried repeatedly to get this resolved without ruffling feathers, but I'm finished trying.

Long before I wrote this letter, I'd learned the art of holding to account the agencies and organizations designed to help. And that it was best done in writing.

It was May 18, 2012. My daughters were in their twenties, preparing to testify in court. They'd been victims of a random gang robbery over a year before while meeting up for drinks with a group of old high school friends. The attack happened in broad daylight, leaving one in their group near death and in intensive care for weeks, and both my daughters with minor physical and major emotional damage.

It couldn't be helped that the trial was scheduled during my youngest daughter's college finals week. But it could be helped that she had just been re-booked by an angry secretary in the DA's office to fly from New Mexico to Alaska during the most inconvenient hours, from an airport far from her college, and with three layovers. The assigned district attorney had ensured her flight was booked as directly as possible, spurring this rogue clerk to return from lunch, shout at the DA, cancel the flight, and re-book it with as many twists and turns as possible.

I had no cause to know about the secretary's employment challenges. Maybe she had personal troubles. Or perhaps she had a close family member pass away. Maybe she was typically nice. I tried to give her an out, but it really didn't matter to me. Because I knew too well about my youngest daughter's health problems, problems made much worse after the robbery. Her sister had already battled serious anxiety and depression. Which is why the girls asked me to help advocate for them, and why the courts allowed it as they were both young adults in need of accommodation. I'd reached out to the clerk directly in writing to no avail. Then to the assigned DA. And now to the top boss and her underling, attaching my prior two emails.

I wish I'd had access to email back when I got my first protective order against my kids' father. Back then, in 1990, it wasn't widely available to the common folk. It was at the shelter when I got schooled on the importance of taking copious notes, so I carried a notebook around.

"The protective order isn't bullet-proof," the advocate told me. "It's fairly useless if you don't know what to do with it, so keep it with you. And every time your husband comes around, you call the police. Even at times when you don't think they'll arrest him. Call in the violation. Ask the dispatcher what the incident number is, and if the police do show up, get the officer's name and badge number. Keep this all in your notebook."

The sum total of documented violations, combined with the fact that I looked like I knew what I was doing, was guaranteed to produce better results than simply crying and falling apart every time there was a violation. Then, if I needed to return to court, I'd have all the history of the protective order listed for the court to consider. And it worked.

This is when I became fanatical about writing things down, and why I want you to do the same. Track the names of people you speak with when in a high-stress situation. You may want to put that name in a search engine online later to find their email. Become that scribe who records your own details, putting a date next to them. Because now that we get to email workers directly rather than fax or call or send a paper letter through snail mail, it gives us many advantages.

You can craft your communication at a time convenient to you, then send it to yourself. Give yourself time to calm down for an hour or a day even. To make sure you're sending the message you're intending, you can have a family or friend glimpse it. And avoid sending multiple emails if one a week could do the trick.

Start the week by sending an email to yourself with a question you'd like to have answered. Maybe the next day, there'll be another, so reply to the original email you sent yourself, and so on. By Friday, you've accumulated three or four. Be sure you look for as much accurate information as you can find on your own.

Remember, the person you're emailing has many other people to serve. Make them want to help you. Spell their name correctly and open the email with a greeting. Do not use exclamation points or all caps or bold all of the text frivolously. It can transmit unintended (or intended) hostility and worse, make you appear absurd. Having a relevant subject line and maintaining a professional tone, even if you feel you know the intended recipient well, is best. And cc others only when necessary.

Once sent, the intended reader can peruse your email at their convenience. And if they do not respond to the call to action (more about that in the next section on How to Craft an Impactful Email), you can forward your original email along with a brief, updated nudge the next time you write. If this produces nothing, forwarding these along with a note to the employee's supervisor is a good next step.

When you're feeling raw, it's easy to assume that not getting an immediate call back or reply to an email is somehow a personal vendetta against you. It rarely is. As a probation supervisor, I've relied heavily on emails from stressed families to keep me informed of both their frustrations and their progress. And sometimes they had to write to me repeatedly if I was too busy, frazzled, or plain disorganized and forgot to respond.

Ask the email designee when you should expect to hear from them. Who their supervisor is. Once you've communicated directly to them without result, and you've refreshed your computer and checked your spam folder to ensure their response wasn't filtered, it's time to use email as your go-to tool of choice.

Just be sure that you wield that tool with caution and move up the ranks of the agency or organization sparingly. As in nearly never.

Ask yourself:

1. Did I leave a clear message with my request in the very first sentence or two, the explanation after, and a small summary afterward?
2. Did I leave a reasonable amount of time before following up?
3. Did I factor in that the employee I'm contacting has multiple other demands on their time?

4. Is there no other person or agency that can help me achieve my goal?
5. Is it time that I contact the supervisor of the employee, summarizing the dates of past efforts and responses, if any? Or should I write to the original employee, cc'ing their supervisor?
6. Did I use the rules of email etiquette?
7. Do I know what my end goal is?

I finished the email regarding my daughters' issues with the pending trial to the supervising district attorney with a call to action:

I've spoken with the Office of Victim's Rights, my own office mates, and will be calling the governor's office by the day's end if this isn't fixed.

... Please fix this mess.

Thank you,

Lizbeth Meredit

I sent that email at 2:08 pm.

And despite the fact that I'd misspelled my own last name (*of course I did!*), I got an emailed apology with the new itinerary hours later. The problem was solved. Permanently. The secretary was removed from her job and re-purposed elsewhere; my daughters made their way through the terrifying process of trial that ended with convictions of all the gang members.

The art of sending emails doesn't solve all problems. If done wrong, it can create more. But it provides an added layer of

GROUNDED IN GRIT: TURN YOUR CHALLENGES INTO SUPERPOWERS

accountability- to you and to the person you're sending it to—a record, and a way for you to sort your feelings and priorities before pressing Send.

Becoming an email maestro helped me not only advocate for myself during times of high-stakes emergencies, it became my superpower during my career. I taught stressed parents in the juvenile justice system the value of email and how to craft them to great impact.

But it sometimes bit me in the butt. If my tone was wrong, if I got too casual with a person I was writing to, or too emotionally invested in a family I worked with, oh, boy.

Early in my career as a probation officer, I got wrapped up in the outcome of a case. I don't remember the details now, but I do remember being furious when disagreeing with an assistant district attorney, a person who I knew personally. Mid-conversation, I hung up the phone on him. Actually, I slammed the phone down. That I remember well.

Instead of calling my boss, which he had every right to do, or calling me right back, which wouldn't have gone well, he sent me a polite, follow-up email:

Dear Liz,

Apparently, your hair's on fire.

Once it's been put out, would you please call me so we can resume the conversation?

Sincerely,

John Parnell

Which leads me to reinforce to you the value of sending a summary email. If you've had a conversation by phone or in person, send a summary email, thanking the worker for their time, a summary of what transpired, and your next steps.

It'll help keep you on track and reduce misunderstandings in case there is a discrepancy between what was said and what the other understood.

In my case, it was a humorous yet sobering reminder that I'd gone rogue, and it'd been noticed. I didn't make that mistake again.

Tip: After you've followed protocols and attempted to get your needs met or conflict resolved without success, your emails may be a critical part of moving accountability to the next level. Sometimes complaining to a governing body like an ombudsman, a commissioner, an executive director may be necessary. Every so often, that's not enough, and filing a lawsuit becomes necessary. No one wants to do that. Yet sometimes it's the only route to success.

Award-winning journalist turned intelligence officer, Suswati Basu, who experiences both physical and mental disabilities, knows too well that systems meant to help don't always without a nudge.

"Holding a system accountable for its injustices is not just about you, it is about the next person that might not make it through this harrowing process."

(Opposite page)

Sample email chain

Dear Mr. French,

Thank you for speaking with me today. I know that you are busy.

I will follow up within five business days to check the status of my application for X. In the interim, I will also gather the documents outlined for our next appointment once my application has been processed.

Should you need to reach me, you've now got my email address in addition to the phone number I supplied.

Thank you in advance for your help.

Sincerely,

Lizbeth

Six days later, a second email that's attached to the original one, forwarded from sent items.

Dear Mr. French,

How are you?

I know you're busy, but I'm checking on the status of my application since it's been six days.

I've done the "homework" you've assigned and am looking forward to hearing from you and scheduling the next appointment.

I'll reach back out in three days if I don't hear back and cc your supervisor in case you're out of town or had unexpected leave.

Sincerely,

Lizbeth

Three days later, the third email with the supervisor cc'd, again with the original two emails underneath, found in sent items. These are clearly fake letters with fake dates. Keep in mind, if you don't have a reason for a deadline, there's no reason to have one. You can simply continue to reach out to the original worker.

Dear Mr. French and Ms. English,

As I referenced earlier, I'm including Ms. English in case you're too busy or out of the office.

I'm checking the status of my application. I'm balancing the fact that my progress feels contingent upon this next step with the fact that you're busy serving others. Any update will be helpful, so I know when to reach out to you again. If I don't hear back within the next three days, I'll call and ask to speak to a supervisor.

Sincerely,

Lizbeth

Tip: When emotions are high, write out the email unfiltered, but send it to yourself and go on with your day. When you return to it hours later, edit it or have a trusted friend edit it for acceptable tone and content. I've never been sorry that I've waited before sending. The same can't be said for when I've pushed *send* under duress.

Resources

Fifteen Essential Email Tips That Every Professional Needs to Know by Gary Stevens

Ten Tips for Writing Professional Emails Rochester Institute of Technology

Reflection

Think about a time when you've needed help from an agency or company. That time when you made phone call after phone call to get some help.

1. How did it make you feel when you couldn't reach a human?

1. Did you give up?

1. Have you ever developed rapport with a person on the other end of the line? If so, how did that impact your experience?

9: Know What You Need, and Tell Your Community

"When I went through my divorce, I couldn't believe who showed up for me," my friend told me over coffee. Her experience is echoed again and again. Ask anyone who's gone through a major life crisis how their friends responded. The memories remain vivid.

"Who showed up for me was not who I expected."

"I was so mad at X during my divorce because I never heard from her."

Romance writer and breast cancer survivor MK Meredith says it perfectly in her memoir, *Not Your Usual Boob*. "Your family and friends will be there as much as they can. They will love you and support you, but not everyone knows how, and not everyone will be comfortable with their own emotions, much less yours."

So true. People in our community are human. Awkward with raw emotions created by traumatic events. And they can't be expected to intuit what we need to hear from them.

"There must have been a reason she was killed," a kind acquaintance responded, after I told her a family member had just been killed by a drunk driver.

Yes. A man drank too much alcohol and got behind the wheel, I wanted to respond. But I knew she meant this in a spiritual context for the purpose of providing comfort.

I should have been used to it by then. What people feel compelled to say in a crisis can be stunning. And it's equally remarkable who shows up. The people you most expect to be there for you may vanish. And friends or family in the periphery may show up, ready to help.

At times, I did mental roll calls of my friends before bed when my girls were kidnapped, cobbling together a list of who I deemed naughty or nice.

Strangers and acquaintances? *Here!*

Coworkers and the grocery store clerk? *Here!*

Friends I saw every day? Crickets.

In hindsight, it wasn't always true. But when I felt raw and alone and indulged in self-pity, this is what I thought back when.

And then I opened my fat trap when the child of a loved one died, and I could not seem to stop myself from saying utterly cringeworthy things.

"How fortunate he was to have you…He's in a better place…"

Why? I asked myself, as I continued to jam both feet in my mouth at once. *You had this training in grad school. Active listening. Just be quiet. Lean into her. Let her know that you're there for her, however she wants that to be. Can you just stop with the platitudes? You're not a human greeting card. SHUT UP!*

Spell It Out to Get the Support You Need

At a book event a few years ago, I heard a writer talk about how she solved the problem. Nadine Kenney Johnstone, author of the memoir *Of This Much I'm Sure,* had struggled with infertility, miscarriages, and in vitro fertilization gone wrong that threatened her very life. She was flooded with unsolicited advice; on adoption, on trying again, on accepting fate. Instead of writhing in disappointment about her support system when the wrong things were said, she elected to make it easy, sending an email with directions. In her book, she wrote, "I ask them to say that they are here for us and are sorry for our loss...With every condolence email that friends send, I feel more supported, less alone."

That's exactly what we need from our friends. To feel less alone. But they're not mind-readers on what we need of them. They're untrained. And even if they are therapists by profession, things are different when they're dealing with someone in their personal life.

Some of my longtime friends contacted me after I published my memoir to say they'd felt disappointed that they hadn't supported me more during different hardships I'd written about. "I never knew," was the resounding message.

I had to stop and think about how that happened. Upon reflection, I hadn't always reached out then to say what I was going through. Part of it was a success. I had reached out for other support. Therapy. Support groups. I journaled sometimes. But some of it was that I avoided being vulnerable. Then I felt hurt by my friends for not being by my side. Yes, sometimes I was the reason that I didn't get the support I needed from them.

Former model and breast cancer survivor/ author Christine Handy admitted that she didn't want to trouble her friends initially when she was diagnosed with an aggressive form of the disease. Her friends weren't hearing it, letting her know that her reaction was selfish. "They wanted to be there for me," she said. "They wanted the chance to carry me if I needed," she said.

It may seem counterintuitive that our not asking for help can be hurtful to our personal supports. I'm certainly not suggesting that their needs override yours, but that they be considered.

Yet if you don't know what your needs are, it's hard to let others know how to help.

Do you know what comfort you need? Is it space, and permission to have time to yourself, putting a temporary pause on normal obligations and routines? Then say so.

My friend Chantelle, an avid reader of John Gray's 1992 classic, *Men Are From Mars, Women Are From Venus*, said she's learned to think of it as crafting a mental job description.

"It's not fair to use our friends as therapists," she said. "So, I like to frame the conversation with, "Do you have five minutes? I'd love to share my feelings with you, but I don't want advice or feedback."

You get the idea. Change the frame if you do want feedback. But the point is, know what you're asking of them and then share it with the person you're seeking support from.

A Sample Email

What I wish I'd had the insight to write, back in the day:

"Dear Friends and Family,

Right now, while I'm working through this period in my life, I'm trying to conserve my energy and am taking a break from emails, calls, and social media. For the next couple of weeks, you won't likely get updates. Please know I feel your support and am simply giving myself time to regroup. If you have a 9-1-1 emergency that you need me for that absolutely cannot wait, please put that in the subject line of your email. Otherwise, I'll be back soon, not back to normal, but more grounded in this journey. I may need occasional prompts from you to reciprocate support, to ask you how you are as I go through this period. I apologize in advance and hope you won't hesitate to let me know when and how you need support, even if I'm temporarily unable to meet your expectations.

Sincerely,

Liz"

If you need to hear from them, let them know. And remember too that if they're part of your personal support, they're impacted by what you're going through also. "Tell those you love how to help," says MK Meredith in her book, "But give them a voice, too. They are going through this right alongside you. They have desires and fears and considerations that need to be met...Make sure you get the love and compassion you need, but also make sure you are giving back to those who make up your life."

Would you like meals delivered? How about a group coffee date with friends? Do you want to receive cards or prayers? Terrific! Share your needs. And share what you don't need. If you want to be heard but don't want advice, say so! Here's another example to mine from:

Sample email #2

"Dear Friends and Family,

I'm hoping this is my rock bottom. Many of you have kindly asked what I need from you, and I appreciate it, even if I can't tell you so individually right now. Prayers, warm thoughts, and eventually, your kind listening ear will be just what the doctor ordered. I'm not looking for advice because it adds to my overwhelm.

Your patience as I muddle through will also be appreciated. I plan on coming back stronger than ever in the end. I just don't know exactly how I'll get there, but I'm thankful to have you, even if you can't always tell.

Sincerely,

(Your name)

Your community of support is worth investing in, and some assertive communication early on can make all the difference between shrinking their numbers or enhancing the connections.

Resources

Of This Much I'm Sure by Nadine Kenney Johnstone

Rallying the Troops: How to Mobilize Your Support by Jennifer Mulder

Reflection

What have people said to you during turbulent times that have been hurtful? How did you feel?

What's been helpful? Has someone shown up in a way that helped you feel supported and less alone?

Have you ever bumbled with your messaging with someone when you meant to provide support or a listening ear?

Can you remember a time you wished you'd reached out to your community but didn't? Draft the letter you wish you'd written.

Part III: Solid Community

10. Rupture and Repair

I received one of the best pieces of advice from a friend when I was in my midtwenties.

"You'll have to learn to schedule your worries," she told me, after I'd nattered on and on about the state of my life. "There are 24 hours a day. You can't let this crisis take over. But if you make a list of things you need to do and put an hour a day on that list for ruminating, worrying, feeling sorry for yourself- all perfectly normal things, then you have 23 more to work with."

It took me a while to figure out why that mattered.

Have you ever known someone who can't seem to talk about anything but their traumatic event, whether it was a breakup of a relationship years ago, a death, or a time they felt wronged?

You know that feeling of dread you get when you see them coming?

Yep. I was that person. In the early days after I'd left my volatile marriage, I could suck the air from the room by unloading the latest drama-filled news when I attended an occasional social gathering.

How do I know?

Another friend told me.

Yes, it was tough to hear at the moment, yet it very likely saved me from tanking the relationships that I'd meant to appreciate and grow.

We can suffocate even the best of our relationships when we forget that the joys and sorrows of others are equally important as our own. And that the systems and agencies designed to help have many other clients, crises, and budget limitations to contend with.

It's hard to remember good social skills when we're hurting. It takes practice. Sometimes, I wrote on my hand, "Ask her how she is!" before I phoned a friend. It was goofy, but it worked. (If you prefer, write it on a sticky note!)

Check in with your confidantes from time to time to ensure they feel appreciated, heard, and valued. It nourishes your garden of support, an irreplaceable part of your path to flourishing.

There are support networks online and in-person groups to help unpack what you're going through. If you can't find one, create it yourself. The value of peer support, of knowing you'll have a space where you're understood, where you can both give and receive support, is empowering. It helped me show up better for my friends and my daughters. And it helped provide a container for my feelings. There was a predictable and healthy outlet. So, when intrusive emotions threatened to take over, I learned to remind myself that it wasn't the time yet. The Worry Hour was coming soon.

It is not about suppressing feelings or pretending everything is all right. It is about devoting time and space to grieve, to rage, to cry, to writhe in anxiety, if need be, and then having twenty-three more hours each day to take good care of you and work through the list of things to be done, including sleep and self-care, of being a human interested in growing your solid support.

Our brains can be reined in and retrained. It takes work, but we can do it. We can stop patterns of ruminating over negative thoughts — the what iffing, the why me, the how will I ever survive this? It's also important that we tune into our feelings, honor them, express them, and not stuff them down.

You're the Boss of Your Feelings

Honoring our feelings, however, is not the same as indulging them. I remember sitting in a huddle of sad and stressed women at the abuse support group in 1990, and thinking it was an odd time to hear the facilitator's gentle reminder: "No one can make you feel anything without your permission."

How was that possible? My husband made me feel like crap, hadn't he? By picking me apart. By his not coming home, night after night, without calling to say where he was. Wasn't he responsible for the hot mess express I had turned into?

No, came her answer. My feelings were my responsibility. Just like my decision to stay or to leave the relationship was my decision.

When you tell yourself, "X (insert person or circumstance) made me feel so bad about myself," you've deemed yourself powerless.

Don't get me wrong, it's important to acknowledge your emotions authentically. We don't need to tell ourselves to just get over it. But it's critical that you understand that it's you and only you who can change how you feel about you and your circumstances.

Want to know more about what I mean? Put *7 Reasons Why the Way You Feel Depends on You* in your computer's search engine. There, writer Kajal Pandey describes how becoming aware of her thoughts and learning to change them had everything to do with finally emerging from a life where she felt victimized and powerless to whatever happened to her.

Our thoughts control our feelings. Our feelings determine our actions. Pandey reminds us that we can choose a better thought.

Example:

I sat at a family reunion in rural Kentucky a few years back after the publication of my memoir. It was my tradition to attend every two years after my kids were grown since it was too spendy to do while solo parenting. This was the first time I'd attended since the book came out.

While much of the family was supportive beyond my wildest dreams, not everyone was. And who can blame them? Writing nonfiction means you're exposing family secrets, hopefully for the purpose of making a point to connect with and help others. But it's still awkward for extended family. And in my memoir, I wrote about my dad admitting to abusing my mother during their marriage, and how, unprompted, he'd taken responsibility for his actions as soon as I met him when I was twenty.

At the reunion, a relative who'd been close to my late father sat next to me. She began speaking loudly to other family members in an exaggerated tone about her unhappiness that I'd written about my dad's actions and gave me the side-eye as she continued. "We didn't consider it abuse back then," she said. "It's just the way it was."

This felt like a personal challenge. She wanted me to engage.

The younger, less aware me would've felt awful. Embarrassed. Sad. Maybe I would have left the reunion. And it

GROUNDED IN GRIT: TURN YOUR CHALLENGES INTO SUPERPOWERS

would've stemmed from the thoughts that I didn't belong, in this family, or in any other.

But now, in my fifties, I recognized the underlying thought. Part therapy, part practice of listening to my inner dialogue and correcting the thinking errors or cognitive distortions, I knew my reaction was based on things that had nothing to do with the situation at hand. I also recognized that my relative wasn't wrong. Historically, men had been expected to rule the roost. Culturally, she had grown up in a tradition that discouraged assertive communication for women, so she likely had no skills with which to initiate a conversation.

I knew my father would have been proud of my book, not just because he loved me, but because it honored his accountability and personal growth.

My relative couldn't make me feel bad so long as I understood my thoughts and reframed them. I chose.

How to feel.

How to behave.

How to proceed.

I had a great day, never engaging in conflict, never talking about the book unless someone asked directly, and feeling thankful I'd finally figured out how to navigate indirect communication in a way that didn't diminish the right to have a difference of opinion with anyone at the gathering.

Taking responsibility for our emotions and responses is the first step to becoming self-aware and empowered.

We have choices. And if we recognize our choices, even though they often come with unintended consequences, we are endowed with how to decide to proceed.

"No one can make you feel inferior without your consent," Eleanor Roosevelt said long ago.

People may treat you poorly. You can't always control that. But they don't have the power to make you feel any kind of way without your consent. They can do things that they know will be hurtful, or helpful. Sometimes they do things without intent. But your reaction is your own. And it's largely influenced by what you allow yourself to think about the situation.

This came in handy when someone pointed out a problematic behavior in me—someone I wanted to keep as a friend.

"That's unacceptable," she told me as we left a toy store after my apocalyptic meltdown.

But was it really? Instantly defensive, I immediately inventoried my justifications:

I was then in the midst of my ongoing and volatile divorce. Being stalked by my now-estranged husband. Living on public assistance and feeling emotionally puny. Dealing with tikes who didn't understand that we couldn't afford the toys they wanted.

So, in turn, I'd shouted at the clerk. Never mind that she'd done absolutely nothing wrong. It was my inability to manage the stress, my inability to accept myself and my current circumstances. It was my problem.

Yes. It was unacceptable. I needed to hear that. I needed to avoid friends who might pat me on the back and tell me not to feel bad. Verbal abuse is never okay, no exceptions. Once we allow ourselves to get a pass due to stress, we've joined the ranks

GROUNDED IN GRIT: TURN YOUR CHALLENGES INTO SUPERPOWERS

of every other abuser who rifles through their pockets to pull out their excuse for why their behaviors were justified.

I had to do better.

And I would. Progress wasn't perfect. But it remained what I continued to strive for.

When I made messes, I had to be held to account. No matter the circumstances. So, I surrounded myself with friends who were assertive communicators. I worked with survivors of tough, tough circumstances who were looking to redefine their futures, and who sometimes looked to me to set the tempo for change.

To this day, when the bottom falls out of my world, and I think that the universe has it in for me, I'll ask myself, "What would you say to your daughters if they were in your shoes?"

Feeling the solid support from others while embracing the need to give back has been pivotal to keeping me grounded.

How (and When) to Apologize

Years after they were grown, my daughters talked to me about times when I'd yelled at them during their childhood. It was scarring, my oldest told me.

This is not how I wanted to see myself.

I bristled. *After all I've done for you*, I wanted to say. *Really? The sacrifices? The opportunities I made sure you had just as kids from two-parent families would? The parenting classes and support groups I took. Therapy. Sports. An optional school program that ate all of my lunch hours to provide transportation. Was I that bad?*

In hindsight, it's easy to see that my kids had never required me to go after some ideal that didn't fit our circumstances. Yes, I'd wanted their lives to not be filled with impediments because I was a single mom. But that choice to fight my feelings of inadequacy fueled monumental efforts that they'd never asked for. They'd have loved to see me relax, to have time for self-care. Take a walk. Journal. Get some rest now and then. Focus more on being and appreciating what we already had.

But hindsight didn't matter now. What was done was done, and for healing to occur, there had to be acknowledgment, apology, and accountability.

Author and writing instructor Laura Davis, who wrote *Courage to Heal* and *I Thought We'd Never Speak Again* has spoken openly about her strife with her mother in the first decades of her life.

While some of the conflicts were typical mother-daughter pains, others were more life-defining. The negative reaction when Davis told her she was a lesbian. The disbelief and denial when Davis disclosed she'd been sexually abused by a relative.

GROUNDED IN GRIT: TURN YOUR CHALLENGES INTO SUPERPOWERS

And yet, as the years passed, both Davis and her mother worked toward repairing the harm. They made baby steps. Rebuilt trust. And focused on their overarching shared goals. By the time her mother died, Davis's mom had accepted that, though hard to have a light shone on past mistakes, the imperfections in their relationship and willingness to share their story made them models for others trying to repair their relationships.

It takes a certain grit to find that kind of courage.

Contrast that with my own mother's decision to send letters to some of her kids more than a decade ago. In it, she wrote (paraphrased) that whatever she'd done wrong, too bad, so sad. "I did the best that I could." She went on to wonder how her children would remember her once she'd died. A shoulder shrug from the woman who told her friends that she had "six ungrateful kids." The implied message: *Get over it.*

It was my mom's accidental gift to me, setting the example I knew I'd need to choose not to follow.

Remember what we talked about in the first section? Parents really are our best educators, good, bad, or mixed. The choice point for us is to assess their impact and become intentional about what we do and don't want to repeat. And then get help making the changes so we don't keep repeating negative patterns. Because an apology is not an apology if it isn't attached to a plan of action to ensure the negative behavior doesn't happen again.

Women often apologize for so many things we shouldn't have to: being assertive, having goals, working while raising kids, not working while raising kids. I read a study once that indicated women have a lower threshold often for why they feel the need to apologize. If you've ever been in a toxic relationship in the past, you may have learned to use apologies as your shield.

So, there's a reluctance today among women to stop apologizing.

I agree that apologizing constantly as a habit isn't beneficial. But that's not what I'm talking about here.

If you've fouled up, and you know or hear that your actions affected another, allow your ego to step aside. Say you're sorry. Let the injured party know what you'll do to ensure it won't happen again. Accountability takes strength. Simply going through the process of that apology will light a fire in you to make good on that vow and build trust between you and the injured party.

Resources

7 Reasons Why the Way You Feel Depends on You by Kajal Pandey

I Thought We'd Never Speak Again by Laura Davis

Persistence U with Lizbeth, episode 86: Laura Davis on Can You Forgive a Parent That You Have a Turbulent History With

Working Conversations by Dr. Janel Anderson, episode 63: Stop Apologizing

Reflection

Have you ever been treated horribly by someone close to you, who then either wanted to pretend the behavior never happened or worse, apologized profusely and begged for your forgiveness, only to repeat the behavior later?

How did you feel?

Did you blame yourself? Wonder if you were overreacting?

When you're stressed, do you tend to turtle up, retracting in your shell and isolating? Or do you use others as sounding boards?

Have you ever chosen not to assertively address a conflict with another person, telling yourself that "it wouldn't make a difference, anyhow?" How has that impacted how you feel about yourself?

How do you feel about apologizing?

11. Fight Isolation and Diversify Your Resources

Once, during my juvenile probation career, I worked with two separate sets of parents whose teens were murdered.

This is likely the worst thing that can happen to anyone, ever.

The first understood that her experience happens far too often. Somehow, that very fact neutralized the situation. Bad as it was, her child's death was not unique. That didn't make it less excruciating. Her only child had died under heinous circumstances. She both felt and shared her emotions. As the offenders responsible for killing her child proceeded to trial, she began reaching out to other families of homicide victims that she met through a victim-serving non-profit to give them support.

The other mother asked, "Why me?" Why was it her child that had been murdered? It was a completely understandable response. The problem was, she got stuck there, and seemed to remain in that mindset permanently. So, why would she reach out for support when she believed she was singled out to suffer? Why would she ever consider speaking with another parent down the road who'd also lost a family member to homicide? Every staff member who touched the case did their level best to listen to her, to connect her to a therapist and other therapeutic or peer-support services.

The last I heard from her, four years after the murder of her child, she wondered aloud what point her own life still held and continued resisting any and all efforts to connect her to services. Her living children had not only lost their sibling, they'd lost their mother. And the rest of the world, including her family, friends, and strangers, would never benefit from her thoughts and experiences—on grief and loss, on the justice system's needed improvements, or anything else for that matter.

Of course, everyone grieves differently. We process crises of any kind through our individual lens. There are no timelines one can be held to, no blueprint that will be seamlessly followed. But going through it in isolation breeds hopelessness.

Carole Brody Fleet, a grief and loss expert and author I interviewed on Persistence U, shared that it was years after becoming a young widow that she began to piece together what would have helped in the early days of loss. "Find somebody who's where you want to be, then latch on. Do what they say."

After navigating those difficult early years, she's enjoyed creating an online community to facilitate supportive relationships with new widows.

Carole encourages anyone to sit in the fog for a while. "Don't try to put a pretty bow on what hurts or feel tempted to tell yourself to just get over it." But, she said, it's important to find community.

"Today is not forever," she reminds us. "Grab on to somebody who can see down the street and around the corner."

How Peer Support Can Change Your World

The opposite of a prolonged period of *Why me?* is the equally detrimental, *I've got this. I don't need any help.*

When my daughter was nearing high school graduation, I couldn't wait to watch her soar. She'd been through so much in her young life. Still, she earned good grades, played soccer, was a cheerleader, and managed to get a scholarship to help with college out of state.

I was both proud of her and ready for her to go away. Especially the latter.

Parenting the girls through their teens was a long slog. They'd done more than their share of rebelling, and I was tired and ill-equipped to manage it. And I'd grown sapped by being needed. I was still young-ish. I had my whole life ahead of me. *Please, God, let me have my Happily Ever After. I've given until it hurts. Make it end!*

Perhaps I should've seen what was coming. Any child who spent two years living in hiding away from their home country after being kidnapped by a parent is bound to have issues with what might feel like a forced separation from a parent.

"Everyone feels anxious the first time they leave home," I reassured my daughter after she began calling, over and over that first month of college. "You'll be fine."

Fast forward a few months. She wasn't fine. And when the final break happened in her brilliant but vulnerable psyche, I could practically hear it from thousands of miles away.

What happened next became part of a new, decade-long struggle that involved case workers, mental health programming, and aid to access medications that cost upward of $1,000 a month.

I'm a consumer of mental health services. I've taken medications to address mood swings and anxiety. I have a master's degree in psychology. But any knowledge or objectivity was gone when it came to my own child. She and her sister are my heart. I'd poured all of my hopes and dreams and plenty of other people's resources into giving them a future that sparkled.

Enter a therapist. Not for her, but for me. I was so very lucky to have already been in counseling back then. My therapist and I merely shifted focus from my issues to how best

GROUNDED IN GRIT: TURN YOUR
CHALLENGES INTO SUPERPOWERS

to deal with hers. I was rigid, anxious, and controlling. None of this was useful or tenable for the long-term good of my daughter or me.

I could count on one hand how many people I'm close to who'd navigated what I was going through. Other well-meaning friends speculated that I might be enabling my daughter by letting her live with me, changed the subject if I talked about it, or struggled with what to say since their kids were doing fine.

But therapy alone, just like relying on a friend or two, can only take you so far. When I joined National Alliance on Mental Illness, NAMI for short, a fabulous resource for families and consumers impacted by mental illness, I got waitlisted for a group that was a game-changer. It wasn't simply the information the facilitator gave. It was the little stuff that the other parents offered. Solutions for how to scale waitlists. Who's the best provider of vocational support? How do you get services for an uninsured adult when there are no agencies accepting a pay- as-you-can system? How do you manage medication side effects? Why do consumers get automatically denied social security benefits the first time they apply?

Never rule out a resource without trying it a few times. Is it embarrassing to find yourself in a peer support group? Sure. Asking for help is humbling. But it's also irreplaceable.

Carol Krein was a retired teacher married for more than 50 years with a close extended family and friendships that span multiple decades. Her social support system appeared to be bulletproof. But when her husband's cognitive and physical health began to take a turn during the pandemic, and the

Veterans Administration denied her husband services, despite his prior military career, she needed more.

Sharing her experience with a friend motivated her to retry the Veteran's Administration. It turned out that there was a pathway to resources that wasn't obvious to the first-time applicant. And then she learned about the local Alzheimer's Resource Center's classes. She asked a trusted friend to care for her husband once a week while she attended a class. The relief was immediate. "I'd always considered the depression he experienced to be a separate issue from the Alzheimer's, but listening to the other people in the group, I learned it wasn't."

But it was more than that. When you attend a peer-support group, sometimes you learn that your concerns, on balance, aren't as bad as they could be. What a relief! Other times, you learn that they're much worse than you allowed yourself to acknowledge, and that spurs on a different course of action.

But perhaps the best part of peer support just might be that all of the imaginary lines that divide us simply begin to fade away. The political ties, religious differences, geographical, cultural, gender, or sexual orientation? When it comes time to roll up our sleeves and get support that will help us flourish, the importance of what separates us diminishes.

It's a takeaway I've found to be sacred after a lifetime of my own troubles. Over time, I came to realize that struggle is universal, and we're living in a world with billions in our extended family.

But I'm not the type to talk to strangers, you may say. *I'm shy*, or *That's just not my thing*.

GROUNDED IN GRIT: TURN YOUR CHALLENGES INTO SUPERPOWERS

You're right. It's a discipline to ask for help. It requires pushing past your feelings of discomfort, of giving up pride, and getting focused.

Adding to your support system will keep you from burning out your current one and will introduce you to people you didn't even know could help transform your life.

And I, for one, don't want you to miss out on them.

Resources

Peer Support: Helping Others, Healing Yourself by Trish Richert

Persistence U Podcast with Lizbeth, episode 33: Carole Brody Fleet on What to Do When Death Do Us Part Comes Too Soon.

Reflection

Have you ever been referred to attend a peer-support group?

Did you attend?

How did you benefit from it?

Did you go back, even when the first meeting was awkward, and you might not have met anyone you could relate to?

If you did not attend, what were the reasons?

Remember, no one will read this but you, so it's okay to be brutally honest.

12. Decluttering the Friendship Closet and Curating the Support You Need

I'll admit it: I adore decluttering maven Marie Kondo and her advice to get rid of belongings that don't spark joy.

It took me many months to sift through a lifetime of belongings when I decided to move across country by myself from Alaska to Tennessee in the middle of the pandemic. I'd been so weighed down by stuff. Cleaning out my closets, tossing photo albums and donating trinkets and clothes that must've been appealing at some point in my life, but that no longer served, made me feel light and energetic. My daughters are grown. I don't need their grade school pictures and report cards any longer. I need to create space for a brilliant future, for new memories and pictures that I'll keep on my smartphone rather than covering my walls with.

But have you ever cleaned out your friendship closet? Have you taken stock of who you spend time with to see if they bring out your best and if you bring out theirs? Do the people you hang out with still fit who you're intending to become, or how you're planning to show up in the world?

I'm proud to have long-term friendships spanning from the early days when I was learning multiplication tables. When your childhood family life is tumultuous, the stability of friendships is extra important. Still, I can't afford to spend time with people simply based on tradition if I'm in a time of transformation or crisis. You can't, either.

Being selective about how and with whom we choose to spend time is crucial. We have limited hours in a day to budget after we take care of our lives, families, and jobs.

I'm a fan of envisioning no more than three different goals or qualities at a time that I intend to master. Then I spend time with those whom I can learn from, or who will hold me to the goals I've said I'm working on. When you're looking to make big changes, it's important to select peer navigators to emulate.

You don't have to lose your current friendship base, but you may need to set limits. Somewhere within your family and friendship group, or at a government agency and faith community, you've got a fixer or a rescuer. Someone who can't wait to get wrapped up in creating your transformation. Their reasons may vary. Some people thrive on others challenges. Emotional vampires. Others are good eggs who wake up every day, wanting to make the world a better place. They may be thrilled to support you and throw money and advice at your problems. "Call, day or night. Whatever you need." And that may be perfectly wonderful, ninety-plus percent of the time. But keep in mind that you do not want to become dependent on any one person, missing the opportunity to develop new emotional muscle yourself. And some rescuers are operating out of their own sense of abandonment. Their need to feel needed can drive their behavior. Once your circumstances improve, or you're no longer in a needy space, the rescuer may be openly resentful, or move on quickly to the next person in need.

How do you know if someone's a rescuer?

Their identity revolves around being needed. While you're listening to their advice, they feel powerful and may put you on a pedestal. The rescuer may try to dominate you with their help, offering it without being asked, and pouting or getting moody when you reject it.

May I make a suggestion? Rather than ignore your feelings of discomfort, speak up. Use your *I* statement. *I feel frustrated when you help me without being asked. I don't want to seem ungrateful, but in the future, please wait until I ask before you offer interventions or advice.*

It's your life. While it's tempting to hand over the reins when it ruptures, you are capable of going through hard times. Once in a great while, you may need to hand over the reins for a discreet amount of time.

But don't abdicate your authority entirely. Handing over your problem and thanking your lucky stars that you've found someone to fix the situation is not the answer. Always remain an active part of your help team. Put in the work for your better future, and it'll inspire others to augment your efforts.

I've told friends during critical times something to the effect of, "Right now, I can only see you once a quarter (or twice a year) given what's on my plate. Don't hesitate to contact me if you need me."

No more explanation than that is needed. Be intentional with your time and who you allow in your circle.

Can This Relationship Be Saved? When It Might Be Time to Say Goodbye

Sometimes, you must cut your losses and move on. If you're leaving a life of substance use, and your former drinking buddy tries to tempt you back to your old ways, leave. If your friend, partner, or family member attempts to control you and keep you small, and talking to that person hasn't produced change, move on.

I moved on from my mother when in my twenties. I saw that she was unwilling to address the underlying issues that led to her being abusive toward her children. "I'm glad I never went to counseling," she boasted in one of our final conversations. "I've just prayed about my problems."

(No offense, God, but it simply wasn't enough.)

My mother was never open to feedback. Never accountable for violence she perpetrated, or the control she exercised to keep us children isolated from one another and from our respective fathers. If you went along with her version of reality, you were a saint. Should you reject it, insert your own opinion, or exercise any sense of empowerment, you were the devil.

I finally cut off all contact when I realized that she was committed to never growing, never changing, never moving forward. When she continued to pick favorite children while ignoring the others, creating a ripple effect of pain in her entire brood. It was never an easy decision, but vital to self-preservation.

I became intentional about who I kept in my inner circle. They need not be perfect. If, in their humanity, they make a mistake and behave ugly or demonstrate a burst of temper (as I have), they would apologize and do their best not to repeat the behavior. Never again would I allow someone to yell, swear, or otherwise frighten me and then pretend later that it had never happened, and that everything was all right.

But that also meant that I needed to not be that toxic person myself. I couldn't expect to have a torrent of emotion and subsequently berate my friends or vent incessantly if I hoped to nurture and sustain a healthy social ecosystem. I'd need to find those other channels to address my problems and attempt to contribute to the relationships that matter.

So, how do you know if your relationships are toxic?

If you leave your shared time consistently more exhausted than when you arrived. If you're made to feel bad for pursuing other friendships, interests, goals, and your efforts to address this dynamic have not produced change. If the other person calls only when they need something. If they're not happy when you prevail after going through a big challenge or achieving a goal, as though your strength is a threat. And if they bring constant drama to your life. Those are a few signs. For more, look at clinician Erica Bonham's post in goodtherapy.com on *Are You a Toxic Person? Ten Questions to Ask Yourself.*

This list of questions applies not just to people in your life, but to you as well:

1. Do you use shaming language?
2. Do you tend to blame others for your problems?
3. Do you try to one-up people who come to you with a struggle or good news?
4. Do you tend to take more than you give?
5. Do you say you don't like drama, but your life is full of it?
6. Do you gossip?
7. Do you fish for attention on social media?
8. Do you complain a lot?
9. Do you dominate the conversation?
10. Are your friends disappearing?

And I would add one more. Do you feel jealous or upset when your friend or partner or child enjoys time with another, certain that you're being intentionally left out, and then act out later?

A client who experienced long bouts of deep depression complained about friends shrinking away after she'd lashed out during an especially rough time in her life.

"Did you ever apologize for your past behaviors to them?" I asked.

"Shouldn't they just know I'm going through something? If they're really my friends, can't they just accept that depression is part of who I am?"

I hope not. Because if they do, everyone loses. There's no equality in that relationship. Nothing to spur better stress management, good communication, or a relationship that gets stronger over time.

Don't get me wrong, you can find people who will allow maltreatment for a time, sometimes for a long time. But in the end, that same person is likely to shoulder it for as long as they can, and then disappear. Even paid professionals in the helping field expect a baseline of courtesy, so while what happened to you is important, how you manage what happened to you is more important.

I didn't manage my own frustrations well enough when my kids were missing, and completely lost my top with an old friend, ruining the relationship. A person can only take so much. So, if the goal is to grow and nurture a strong and supportive community, assess how you're showing up with people who care about you and who serve your needs. Review the list above and reroute when necessary.

Cultivating Relationships that Blossom

It's also critical to celebrate the relationships that give you energy, that increase your motivation to make good choices, that urge you to be your best self. Someone who accepts you as you are while fully anticipating the all-you-will-be later and isn't threatened by your amazing capacity.

Do you feel emotionally and physically safe when you're together? Would they say the same about you? These are the relationships to prioritize. And the toxic ones? Until you're feeling strong enough to change the dynamics, these are the ones to downgrade, at least temporarily.

Picture yourself as a flower in a garden. Which relationships inspire you to blossom? Which will you continue to water and fertilize? And which are like weeds, destroying the rich soil around you, suffocating your growth?

It's time to prune those relationships.

Resources

Are You a Toxic Person? Ten Questions to Ask Yourself by Erica Bonham

Reflection

Give your closest relationships an honest assessment.

What relationships are toxic, and why?

Which relationships are problematic but worth trying to save?

Which relationships inspire you to blossom?

13. Aligning Your Values

"Why don't you apply for a Pell grant to help you finish college?" asked the court-appointed guardian ad litem, whose sole job was to decide what was in the best interest of my then-small children. In my midtwenties, I'd made the bold move to leave my volatile marriage. And in doing so, plunged my children and me into a world of begging for public assistance and a life in low-income housing. While I'd already taken the nudge to enroll in college, I didn't know how I would pay for it.

"I can take out a loan," I responded weakly, trying hard to block the feeling of despair as I thought about how much student loan debt I was already in from my prior failed effort at college.

"But why would you?" she asked, her voice softening. "A Pell grant is something you wouldn't have to repay."

Why would I allow myself to cascade into debt when I didn't have to? That was easy.

There was someone out there far more deserving of getting free money from the government. Lots of someones. Who was I to stick my hand out again? I was already on food stamps, living in low-income housing. Legal Aid assigned me a paralegal to assist with restraining order proceedings. Wasn't that bad enough? I felt like a pimple on the face of the earth.

"You know," the guardian ad litem continued, "the government doesn't offer free help without a motive." She went on to explain that by finishing my education instead of grabbing two different jobs at minimum wage as I'd planned, I would pay higher taxes for the balance of my career. "You'll be a much greater asset to the government if you have your degree. And you'll be less likely to bounce in and out of poverty. You can support your family and create a real future."

I barely heard the second part. All I could think was *The government had a motive?* It had never occurred to me that handouts were an investment, not a giveaway. I could be an asset for life to my family and the world around me. Maybe it was obvious to everyone else. But not to me. And with the realization, two things happened:

One, I began to get a vision of me giving back. Me with a good job and paying those higher taxes. Me volunteering one day in addition to having meaningful work. And me, parenting two young women who would have access to education.

Two, I had a lightbulb moment regarding accepting help. It wasn't simply that the government had a motive. It was the realization that everyone does, including family and friends and strangers. They might not recognize it themselves. But there is a drive, a mission, a motive behind what others do for us. Your awareness of this when asking for help makes it much easier to make clear-minded choices.

Asking yourself what the motive may be will help you decide if it aligns with your goals and aids you in setting boundaries. It may lessen hurt feelings and misunderstandings later. It may also alert you to how you can give back down the line, or what improvements you'd like to see made for others who'll one day be in your shoes.

While I don't recommend asking individuals why they are willing to help as it may come off as rude or put the helper on the defensive, I do recommend checking out faith communities and agencies online to become familiar with both their history

GROUNDED IN GRIT: TURN YOUR CHALLENGES INTO SUPERPOWERS

and purpose. It can reduce surprises and explain how resources are allocated. Making a habit of doing this early on can remove some of the unknowns. And when you're living in unexpected chaos, every bit of calm you can create helps.

Take an honest look at your support network. Do you think that your family and friends can extend themselves and remain neutral, without having any expectations of you? Government, churches, and non-profit agencies also follow their mandates.

Let me give two examples.

Megan was a former domestic abuse victim who insisted she didn't need help from anyone but her church. It sounded terrific, until the church wanted to influence her decision about whether to return to her husband. "They think he's better now," she said guardedly.

Sarah cared for her diabetic father for years after complications rendered him disabled. She was relieved when her father told her he'd already filed both his will and a do-not-resuscitate order with the courts. When she rushed her father to the local Catholic-run after a massive stroke, her father's advanced directive was ignored. He was furious upon waking up after a prolonged coma, yet the hospital's stated mission is to preserve life.

None of this should foreclose the opportunity to reach out for and appreciate the support offered. Asking yourself what the person or agency's mission and purpose may be can help you decide if it aligns with your goals, or if the cost of getting the support is too great. It puts you back in control. Even if your options each come with conditions, you'll be choosing which ones you can live with. And if the conditions are too great, where else can you find that will offer similar help?

Ask yourself:

What is the mission of this person or resource? What are their expectations of you, the recipient of services?

What about the person offering direct help? How well do you know them? Are there boundaries that need setting? Are they offering so much support that you feel suffocated, resentful, or uneasy? Do you find yourself abdicating your own sense of power to them, letting them do the heavy lifting that you know deep down you are capable of?

Help Them Want to Help You

"What do you mean I can't get pain and suffering for my child's anxiety?" an angry mother of an assault victim screamed at the district attorney in a telephonic planning meeting. We were preparing for a sentencing hearing of a juvenile suspect. This was the third attempt at bringing the request for restitution down from the millions of dollars requested to the potential thousands it might take in future therapy bills to reduce the emotional damage of the boy he'd threatened. It's worth repeating that there were no physical injuries. The victim's mother had been repeatedly advised that she could pursue pain and suffering through civil courts, advice she appeared to forget.

"Do you mean I have to spend money to get this done?!!! My son is *SCARED*!" she bellowed.

It was sad, yes. But it wasn't a productive use of energy. It did not help her son's case. It didn't help the relationship between her and the parties who were pursuing compensation

GROUNDED IN GRIT: TURN YOUR CHALLENGES INTO SUPERPOWERS

on her son's behalf, and I can only imagine that it did little to combat her own feelings of helplessness and overwhelm.

When your life feels like it's reached an all-time low, it's hard to hear that you're still responsible for how you respond to it. You may want to scream and shout and throw yourself on the ground, writhing in agony.

After leaving my violent marriage, a friend gave me important advice: "Make everyone know you're special. The world is filled with billions of people. Help people know who you are and why they should care...Make them want to help you."

Back then, I was deeply angry about having no safety. No money. No help with my tiny tots. Had I allowed myself to regularly show my true emotions to the public, I'm certain I would have been arrested.

So, instead, I collected names, phone numbers and kept them in a notebook. Had email been widely available back then, I'd have collected that, too. I tried to arrive at appointments prepared and wrote down what I was tasked to do before our next appointment. If a person or provider suggested I access an additional referral, I listened, because it helped to me get prioritized as a client.

If I was on my A-game, I remembered my manners, and asked how the worker was doing. And, once email was invented, I sent a quick note to confirm what we'd discussed after appointments or telephone conversations. That way, I could look them up in sent items, or keep the email collection in a specific folder when I misplaced my notebook.

I didn't always succeed, but here are a few tips I learned by trial and error:

Make a positive connection with at least one staff member.

Go at it like you're looking for a new best friend. I'm exaggerating a little, but at each agency you rely on for support, it's important to get to know the staff. Get his or her name. Ask for their email address. And be courteous, no matter how stressed you are, no matter how stressed they are. It is your need that is being met, so act accordingly. That doesn't mean you need to accept abuse or sloppy work, but remember that the number of people needing help always exceeds existing resources.

Questions to ask during your first appointment, or afterward as an email follow-up.

1. How soon can I expect to hear from you?
2. Which is your preferred method of contact?
3. Have you any advice for me to make your job easier?
4. Who is your supervisor or work partner, in case you're away and I need to get information more quickly?
5. Is there something you'd recommend I do before the next time we speak?

Remember to commence by thanking them for their time, closing written communications with your name, email address, and phone number.

Anything to demonstrate that you are on your details, want to partner with them, and are tracking progress.

I had to remember that no matter my frustrations, the staff had the ability to meet my needs. I was not meeting theirs. You might say, "But it's their job to be nice to me, to help me. They're the professionals."

True. But now, after a long career as a public servant, I can tell you from experience that workers will prioritize serving those pleasant to deal with who are receptive to feedback, who put more energy into solving their own problems than dropping them at the feet of a stranger. They'll find partnering with you to be meaningful, and consider time spent to be a worthwhile investment not just for you, but for their agency as well.

Follow Through for the Long Game

I was retrieving my voicemail at work on a Monday morning, when I heard from the mom of a victim of dating violence. We'll call the mom Donna. She'd been left as the point of contact after her daughter received a brain injury from a severe assault by her estranged boyfriend. A quick search of records indicated Donna's daughter was now twenty, and it had been two years since we'd last connected.

"Hi," she said, "Long time, no hear."

I called Donna back as I pulled up my old file notes. During our last contact, I'd compiled a comprehensive list of referrals that could help her daughter, sitting alongside her to call a few of the referrals, arranging appointments together to make things easier.

Now, as Donna gave me an update—that the young man was released from a treatment program, that he'd found a new girlfriend to abuse, that when said girlfriend went underground for protection, he returned his attention to his original victim- I reviewed the old to-do list.

"I just don't know what to do," Donna said.

Should she call the police? Get a new order of protection? Move her daughter out of state?

None of these were decisions I could make for her, or her daughter.

"Have you two contacted the women's shelter as I'd recommended to speak with their court advocates? Or gone in for a support group there so your daughter could compare how other people have navigated safety planning?

"Did you call the police's domestic violence unit and establish rapport there and get them familiar with your daughter's story?

"Did you contact the victim-serving agencies that can help with counseling referral costs?"

No on all fronts. They had done nothing during the twenty-four months since we'd last spoken, naturally assuming that once the former boyfriend had been arrested and later found a new victim, there would be no need to get help.

"What should I do?" she repeated. It was clear she was dropping the problem at my feet.

I rubbed my temples, trying to will my judgment away. What I wanted to say was, "I will never invest more energy into the problems of another person than they do themselves. Part of recovery is learning to ask for help. It's creating a relationship with the professionals who can help and giving and receiving support in groups with people going through similar challenges.

There is no one right answer that will produce a perfect result for any of our problems. But there is definitely a wrong way to approach a crisis: Do nothing. Wait for someone else to take control. Allow the problem to fester and create a second and a third."

I sent the referrals again and wished her well, explaining that I had no jurisdiction over the problem since all parties aged out of the juvenile justice system. "The same referrals I made two years ago can help you both now. Otherwise, I'm worried that the pain of the assault won't lessen over time."

I knew I may as well have been speaking Swahili. Donna and her daughter weren't looking for a comprehensive approach. They were looking for safety in the short term.

Getting through each catastrophe as an isolated event, like it's simply one big bad stroke of luck, rather than playing the long game—investing the time and energy to get the information and support necessary, all but ensures there will be no personal transformation that will inspire growth and development. While it's easier, and decidedly more comfortable, my wish for you is to develop emotional muscle.

If the bottom has fallen out of your world, and your reflex is to run to one go-to friend or family member or agency, over and over, you've got a recipe for disaster. Of being too dependent, or burning out your friend or family member, or burning through a resource that could, for one reason or another, go away.

My favorite recipe for success is still a combination of support from agencies and non-profits, a local support group or online forum, therapy or coaching when needed to manage my response to the trauma, and the self-care tips including the Worry Hour that I told you about before.

With limited resources available, initiating recovery and following through with services offered is the way to get taken seriously for future aid. Showing up, even when things have stabilized, when the emotional roller-coaster is (for now) over will empower you with information, support, and give you a good credit score with those intended to help.

I had another client we'll call Adella. I'll tell you more about her soon. She was the Anti-Donna. Advocating for her deaf child with psychotic symptoms, English, her second language, a budget so tight it squeaked. Yet she persisted. She made people like her. She showed up prepared. She followed through with recommendations without fussing that she was too busy or too exhausted, though both were true. And she made email her tool of choice. She learned to move mountains with far fewer resources available to her than most of us, including Donna.

Showing up consistently and accessing a variety of support helps siphon at least part of the pain from your emotional wound. And it demonstrates that you're in the driver's seat of your journey.

The Power of a Thank You

"Did you contact Mr. Betts to thank him yet?"

I could almost hear my oldest daughter's eye roll from her bedroom. Glancing at my to-do list as she readied in the bathroom for her new job at the mall, I wasn't looking to start an unnecessary battle. But Mr. Betts, her vocational rehabilitation technician, had been a miracle worker, and he deserved to hear a success story.

Getting a job had seemed like a permanent impossibility when my daughter was first diagnosed with serious mental health problems. I would never have guessed that she would later go on to complete a college degree. Back then, basic life skills had to be relearned. A cocktail of just the right doses of medications needed perfecting. Therapy to touch on the many new losses this newest setback would bring to her life. It took well over a year before she was ready to go to vocational rehabilitation.

Of all the government agencies I've been a consumer of, vocational rehabilitation wins for being the smartest, good for taxpayers, good for clients. They insisted that she demonstrate initiative before investing in her, offered small incentives, spent resources doing testing only after she'd established her seriousness in creating a better future. And now, years in, she was employed.

> "That's what a case manager does," my daughter shrugged. "He won't care."

Normally, I wouldn't concern myself in the affairs of an adult child, but this was different. I was a partner with my daughter in her recovery, and was in semi-regular contact with Mr. Betts, so I pushed back on the point. He needed to hear that his work made a difference.

Thank you. This simple phrase can change not just the trajectory of someone's day but has the power to change lives.

It's also something workers who serve the public don't get enough of. But they should. Yes, they are doing their jobs and being financially compensated. But the power of thank you is that it not only breathes new energy into the person being thanked, but often that energy is paid forward with a renewed passion and commitment for doing the job. And both government and non-government organizations routinely use those thank you's, those stories of success, in the applications for grants and other resources.

If you've not seen it already, watch the Thank You Project video by Kellie Haddock at www.kelliehaddock.com/home/the-thank-you-project. Haddock was a young, happily married mother with a newborn son when a car accident claimed her husband's life and put her baby boy in jeopardy. Ten years later, she made it her mission to connect with the medical team and even the helicopter pilot, every person who was involved in saving her son's life. One member of the team commented that in her career, she'd never been thanked after a traumatic incident by a survivor. I challenge you to watch the video and not tear up.

This isn't just me as a retired government worker talking. Or me as a person who's had cause to work with more agencies and resources than I'd care to think about over my lifetime to address various and sundry problems. The benefit of saying thank you is well-researched.

In 2010, two researchers named Grant and Gino confirmed that not only does expressing gratitude make the recipient feel good, but it doubles the odds that the thanker is helped again by the helper he or she is thanking. It increases the chances that a future help-seeker is served And a side benefit? The enhancement of pro-social skills for you, the person who may feel sheepish about asking for help in the first place. It's inspiring to give back. And your thank you is definitely a way to give back.

How do I know?

At the end of my twenty years working in probation, I received a thank you from a mom of a juvenile probationer. It was long and heartfelt, something I keep saved now at my home office to inspire me. In part, she said, "I'm glad I was able to have you in our lives during our difficult situation. I would not have wanted anyone else. I learned so much. You gave me the push when I needed when I thought everything was lost and didn't know how to even start to get help...I will always remember you."

Seriously. Someone wrote that. It still makes me emotional. In a job I'd often loved, but that never loved me back, those words still bring joy.

"Dear Mr. Betts," her letter began. And my heart swelled, thinking how pleased he would be to hear from her.

Go ahead and include a worker or a stranger you've come in contact with through your period of personal pain, and then formalize that gratitude in writing.

And think of how paying it forward is already helping to change lives besides your own.

Resources

The Thank You Project video by Kellie Haddock at www.kelliehaddock.com

Why Thank You is More than Just Good Manners by Jeremy Dean

Reflection

Have you ever sought help from an agency, only to have them refer you to one or two others before they would help? What did you do?

Did your experience working with outside resources spur you to want to volunteer or find professional work in that same field?

Think about a time when a professional you worked with went above and beyond. How did you express your gratitude? If you haven't, can you find their email or connect through LinkedIn and send a thank you?

Part IV. STUBBORN PERSISTENCE

14. The Crisis Makeover

"How did you do it?" I asked Adella about her total transformation from family doormat to fierce mother and advocate for her child. Adella was the mother of a delinquent youth who frequented our detention center for years when she wasn't in residential treatment centers.

But by now, I hadn't seen Adella's daughter in many months. She was living back at home, had a new, healthy peer group, and attended school in the community. And she was crushing every bit of it.

Adella beamed and gave a quick shrug.

"Don't be modest. You're an inspiration," I told her. "I'm going to write about you one day."

Adella's child wasn't typical of youth in the justice system. She was deaf. She didn't know how to sign, nor did any of her family. She was experiencing psychosis, even hearing voices. And Adella's family, which consisted of her and her husband and two other grown kids, spoke English as a second language. They'd never learned to sign. Adella and her husband worked opposite shifts in jobs that barely paid the bills, with nothing left over for expensive interventions her child would need.

From a traditional Hispanic family, the care of this teen had fallen squarely on her small shoulders.

"How did this happen?" I'd wanted to ask when Adella first told me that the family hadn't known their daughter was deaf until she was well past toddlerhood. How was it that after they found out, no one in the family learned to sign? How was it that the family had subsequently allowed Adella to bear the brunt of the burden of this girl's care, when clearly her needs necessitated that of a village?

I suspected a lot of the answers were likely wrapped up in issues of culture and gender expectations, a lack of resources, and other family dynamics. And by now, the *whys* didn't matter nearly as much as what could be done about it.

Adella was tasked with the impossible. How does one advocate for their child with disabilities when the child can't communicate what's going on, and when the parent did not yet fluently speak English? How does a hardworking mom continue to show up for her job when her daughter has been up all night long, banging on the walls and turning up the radio to maximum volume, subjecting this hardly-getting-by family to homelessness should their landlord evict them?

When I first met Adella, there were dark circles under her eyes. She shifted uncomfortably and avoided eye contact. Her body language indicated an apology to the universe for her existence. I wondered who she had been before she became a wife, a mother, and the last person on her list of priorities. Her daughter frightened her, other family members tread upon her, and those of us working in the human services field- including me- doubted her capacity to manage all of the moving pieces she had to juggle. Yet despite all of the barriers, it appeared that she was willing to do whatever it took to be an agent of change.

Adella was open to trying the mix of interventions that had worked for me. Becoming a student of the issue she faced. Joining an advocacy group. Benefiting from peer support. Getting support from a therapist at the community mental health center. And giving back to others going through similar circumstances. It was a multi-pronged solution that few who wanted quick results would sign up for.

Adella called a lot that first year, asking the government to step in and provide respite or to make decisions and set limits with her child that most parents manage themselves. "My daughter refuses to get up and go to school...She threw her cell phone across the room and it broke. Now she's asking for another..."

She wanted her daughter to be held accountable for bad behaviors, but she didn't want to be the one doing it lest her child retaliate. Under the guidance of an amazing clinical team at work, our office gave referrals to her family.

She followed through. Agencies that served the hearing community refused to help. Nothing appeared to change. Adella felt despondent. She wanted to quit. But she doubled down. More recommendations and referrals came. She took them. Nothing appeared to change.

More recommendations and referrals. She kept working with them. It became clear that the problem wasn't simply that she had a deaf child who experienced mental health problems. It was the isolation Adella experienced as a parent. The shame. The discomfort about asking for help.

Still, Adella persisted. Calling strangers at agencies she'd never heard of. Getting on waitlists for resources. Mastering new parenting techniques. Even taking a self-defense course to increase confidence when dealing with her blow-outs. In time, around 36 months, to be exact, everything changed.

Confidence Beyond Crisis

All told, she followed up with at least seven different referrals. There was no service suggested that she refused to try. And once her husband and other kids began to see the payoff, they joined her efforts. Each member of the family stepped up more than ever to play a role in the solution.

I got an email from Adella, who cc'd six more people from the various agencies she'd engaged. In the email, she kindly yet firmly requested help getting her daughter lifelong support. She would still live in the home until adulthood, but Adella's daughter would need a case manager who provided access to services and support. The email was both pointed and polite. Each recipient responded quickly to her call for help. Adella had nurtured a relationship with all of the different agency representatives. She'd earned their favor by demonstrating that she was a powerful participant in her child's life. This mother had found the key to unlock support.

But the confidence she gained while knocking down barriers? That confidence didn't just follow her when dealing with the people helping with her daughter. It came to work with her, resulting in a promotion. It showed up in her personal life, where self-care became sacred, and she dropped a couple of dress sizes. It showed up in her marriage, where the division of labor appeared to re-settle to something more balanced, where there became room for personal development in addition to being a wonderful mom, a great wife, an inspired worker.

Crisis didn't define Adella. It refined her, transforming who she was and how she showed up in her life.

When I gave her props, Adella simply deflected. "I feel so lucky to have found the right support at the right time," she said.

"But what do you think is the key to your success?" I nudged. "Was there a point in which it simply all clicked?"

Adella couldn't answer that. I should've known better than to ask.

The one thing about triumphing through crisis is that there's no one thing. Success could never be premised on one. One friend. One therapist. One agency. There would need to be a number of different resources that locked together like pieces of a puzzle in order that when one friend or mentor moved away, when one agency lost funding, when one source proved ineffective, there was still a safety net of care. Interdependence spread evenly, not a pretense of independence, as humans need one another to survive, or overdependence on a single provider of relief.

In the end, Adella was forever changed. She never attempted to take credit for her daughter's progress. But she has become a fierce advocate for her child, and in the process, has become her own as well. She now takes care of herself and extends the compassion she'd long given everyone in her world to herself as well. She doesn't hear the word *no* from anyone and let it deter her. She finds workarounds. Her energy isn't constantly drained by that sense of shame that lies to us by telling us that we should be able to manage life's predicaments on our own. She asks for help with confidence. And she is happy to talk about her experiences and to help others when presented with the opportunity. She can reach for and provide help as needed. Adella sparkles with both pride and a sense of her purpose.

Imagine how great you will feel when you look back at the hardships you've been through, knowing they helped you become the enhanced version of yourself.

15. How has the Journey Changed You?

June 30, 1979, Writer James Baldwin in his letter to agent Jay Acton:

...a journey is called that because you cannot know what you will discover on the journey, what you will do with what you will find, or what you will find will do to you.

"It feels like a low-grade depression I just can't shake," I told my friend Ann at dinner. "I've plowed through so many of the goals I'd set for myself. The girls are all but grown. And I feel dreadful."

If only things were different, I had once told myself and Ann back in the day when my life was in shambles. *I'd be so happy if I could create a predictable life. If I could have reliable transportation. A salary in which I could afford food, my mortgage payment, and utilities without having to stagger which bills I paid. If I could create that life, I'd never complain again.*

And yet here I was, complaining. I'd been working in a union government job, finally able to provide the girls medical insurance. I'd finished graduate school, no longer balancing work, kids, school, and a paper route. Shut-off notices from the utility companies were no longer affixed to my door. The girls were earning good marks in school and were involved in other activities. I had dates when I wanted and maintained soulful relationships with friends and with a growing number of family members. I had everything (I thought) I'd ever wanted.

And I was miserable.

Sometimes it's because us goal-getters have a twisted belief that once we've achieved what we've meant to, a magical shift will happen. *If I could only get _____, then my life would be better.*

Sometimes we've simply chased the wrong goal. But for me, more than anything, it turned out that I subconsciously missed the struggle.

Looking back, I should have expected the plummet. I was native to the land of calamity, and an immigrant to the ordinary life I'd achieved. My identity had been hinged on overcoming. When that period ended, I wasn't sure who I was or where the real me had gone. I felt like an impostor. I felt twinges of survivor's guilt for leaving hard times behind.

Additionally, I'd grown complacent. I'd wanted the chance to pursue dreams of my own that I'd set aside to raise a family. I wanted to finally publish the book I'd been chipping away on for nearly two decades but had failed to get an agent or publisher. It seemed the industry had all but given up memoirs of non-celebrities just when I made it to the finish line.

I wanted to travel. Not to easy destinations like Las Vegas or Hawaii. I wanted to see far-flung continents, hear foreign languages, eat the native foods. Yet somewhere along the way, I resigned myself to the fact that since I was neither young, rich nor coupled, big travel was out of the question. (Talk about serious thinking errors!) And subconsciously, when I gave up on my dreams, I began feeling like a victim. Again.

Yet it isn't just people leaving volatile circumstances that are prone to needing electrifying stimulation. Thrill-seeking or scouting out different stimulation, has a function in all of our lives. "It gives us the opportunity to focus on one thing at a time," says psychologist Marvin Zuckerman, PhD.

GROUNDED IN GRIT: TURN YOUR CHALLENGES INTO SUPERPOWERS

"Our early ancestors survived by hunting and food gathering," he explains. "Hunting was one of the early expressions of sensation-seeking, particularly when they began to hunt large mammals where there's a high risk involved...Back then, it was a matter of survival. In today's far safer world, it's a matter of pleasure."

I'd not found myself to be a thrill seeker when I had no power in my world.

Whether you've lived a life of extreme highs and lows like me, or you've finished a long period of hardship, you just might have a sense of loss when it ends. I saw it with juveniles on my caseload who successfully kicked substance abuse, and with domestic violence survivors who occasionally traded in one abuser for another. Their brains were still wired for chaos. I don't believe anyone enjoys the punishing impact of substance use or domestic violence. But, a hidden part of us may miss the familiar sense of drama a crisis provides and gravitate toward the familiar rhythms of what we know. The adrenaline rush. And I hate to admit it, but even the sympathy often afforded us during setbacks is part of the allure that disappears once we successfully stabilize our lives.

Therapist Rita Barsky put it best in her blog when talking about adults from dysfunctional homes who subsequently struggled with addiction and who railed against the calm. In her 2007 blog post, *A Sober Mind: Addicted to Chaos*[1], Barsky noted, "They never felt safe in their family of origin and the only thing they knew for sure was that nothing was for sure. Life was totally unpredictable, and they became conditioned to living in chaos."

---

1.   http://asobermind.blogspot.com/2007/12/addicted-to-chaos.html

There are problems in not recognizing the signs of what she's called chaos addiction. Those used to chronic chaos become anxious in the unfamiliar tides of calm and wait for the other shoe to drop. And they may find themselves drawn to the problems and chaos of others around them, happily reveling in the details and plunging headlong into becoming part of the solution.

Reevaluate Coping Strategies

Bless their hearts. Coping strategies, those defense mechanisms, habits, and behaviors that we've allowed to protect us during periods of turbulence, often hold tight onto us, long after their benefits have expired.

Some of us may have taken solace in Jack Daniels or Louis Vuitton during long periods of stress. Others may have used a technique like the Worry Hour, only to find that we're compartmentalizing our feelings to our detriment well after our dark season has passed.

It reminds me of when we begin a new weight loss plan. We don't mind trying a new way of eating at first. Of moving our bodies more. Our vision toward health and fitness is crystal clear. Maybe the goal is to feel good by a certain special event or holiday. Maybe it's a class reunion, or to get back to pre-pregnancy weight. And once the pounds start to melt, the fact that we're tiring of this more restrictive way of life is initially muted by the compliments we receive. This can carry us a long way, sometimes long enough to reach our goal. But then we learn the hard realities about weight maintenance, like the fact that sustaining the weight loss will forever be a process that requires ongoing attention and efforts, or we'll go right back to old patterns and eventually, to our former, less healthy shape.

It's up to you to look at habits and behaviors that have helped in the past. Do they honestly serve you now, or are they multiplying old problems and creating new ones?

For example, when I was in the thick of trying to restructure my life and leave chaos behind, I knew I had to implement routines and disciplines. I had to stop, as an example, letting my small kids decide when they were tired enough to go to bed at night. I had to stop letting whether I enjoyed exercise determine whether I did it.

Sounds good in theory, right? The new mindset shift helped me and the kids eventually move forward, accomplish goals, and gain a semblance of organization.

But I became rigid when it came to changing up our plans. Even our fun times became events that I tried to choreograph. And do you know what works horribly when parenting teenagers? Operating the home like a boot camp. I had to completely reroute and let go of some of the things that before had served me or us a family.

Remember to reroute from time to time. Use both the self-compassion and thinking errors information to determine if what worked for you in the past should continue to accompany you further to your new future.

Combatting Strivers Remorse

"So, now what's the plan?" I asked the teen we'll call Sandy, who'd just received her high school diploma. I was at work in juvenile probation, conducting an office visit to check on her progress in meeting the final goal that Sandy and her probation officer had crafted together. At work, we called them case plans.

The goals were both a consequence for committing a crime and intended to target the factors that led to it to work toward preventing future offenses.

Sandy looked back at me with a blank expression. I could tell what she was thinking (thanks to decades of working with delinquent youth). *What? Wasn't graduating enough? Does there always have to be something else?*

Good question. Why do we need to have another goal lined up? Can't we just reach our destination and rest a moment?

Just my opinion, but I think it's important to rest a moment. We need to congratulate ourselves, do a happy dance or reward ourselves in a way that won't set us back, and then answer a few questions about the process.

What did it take to follow through? What new skills did you gain? What sacrifices did you make to achieve success?

Which is what I asked Sandy. She wrinkled her forehead and looked down at her feet. Then she looked up at me, eyes brightened. "I had to sit in the front of class, which made my best friend mad. And then I realized that she always gets mad when I do well. So, we're not friends anymore."

Wow. Now that's insight.

I'm a huge believer in finding that next goal after achieving the first one. Life doesn't stop once we've reached a destination. It's a journey. Let's keep it moving.

Sometimes, there's a feeling of emptiness that accompanies reaching a goal. I call it striver's remorse. We've been so focused, so strategic, and now, we're done.

We feel a high after reaching our goal, but then comes a very natural *Is this it?* sort of feeling. And since our

GROUNDED IN GRIT: TURN YOUR
CHALLENGES INTO SUPERPOWERS

expectations of how achievement will make us feel are often unmet, we slump.

According to writer Wanda Thibodeaux of Inc. Magazine, "The brain releases dopamine, a hormone associated with both motivation and happiness, *in anticipation of* reward. So, when you plan and know you're going to work for something, you're in a biological position to feel good. Each milestone gives you another dopamine hit, which makes you want to keep going with the job. But when you reach your goal, that release of dopamine drops. It's harder for you biochemically to have joy."

That isn't only challenging for juvenile delinquents. For any of us with mood disorders, substance abuse challenges, or are hardwired to seek adventure, this is big. Anticipating, planning ahead so there is a goal in the future—is it guitar playing? Walking 1000 more steps on most days? Saving $100 a month from living expenses and investing it? -it's empowering to have that next goal at the ready.

For teenaged Sandy, her choice fit her circumstances perfectly. "I'm meeting with a recruiter," she said a few days later by phone. "I can have a fresh start and learn new skills if I join the military. I don't have money for college, and I don't want to start life in a bunch of debt. And I can get away from my peer group."

Touché! And just like that, Sandy became the young woman with a plan.

For some of us, going to vocational school or college can be that goal, the next thrill. Nothing says you're falling off a cliff quite like finals week. But for others, it may be joining a boot camp of sorts, or attending a Toastmaster's meeting for the first time, or perhaps investing in a foreign language course.

I knew that Sandy would not stagnate. Last time she called, she was living on a military base in North Carolina. Planning to enroll in college.

Shortly afterward, I followed her lead and booked a solo trip to Vietnam and Laos. Which has led to multiple other solo travel trips that have spanned six continents so far, and sparked the confidence needed to finally publish my memoir.

As I booked my first hostel, I realized that living in a shelter briefly, followed by years of self-denial to get out of poverty, had uniquely qualified me to travel on a budget. Rescuing my kidnapped daughters had taught me to land on my feet when things went sideways in a country where I didn't speak the language. Decades of peer-support experiences greased the wheels for me to make lasting connections with other travelers and people native to the lands I traversed.

Author and podcaster Anu Verma also found travel to be a newly discovered form of bliss. After leaving childhood abuse behind, followed by narcissist abuse in an adult, intimate relationship, she said her desire to escape took her on two backpacking trips around the world, including skydiving in Cairns, and volunteering in schools in Nepal. "If it weren't for my abuse and my need to leave it, I might never have developed my love of travel," she said.

Travel, especially extreme, low budget international travel, is not everyone's dream. Neither is writing. But what *is* yours?

Resources
The Science of the Thrill, Atlantic Magazine
I Am Not Your Negro by James Baldwin

Rita Barsky 2007 blog on BlogSpot: A Sober Mind: Addicted to Chaos.

Neuroscience Says This is The Most Powerful Way to Reward Yourself by Wanda Thibodeaux

Persistence U Podcast with Lizbeth, episode 35: Anu Verma on Pushing Back Against Gender and Cultural Norms.

Reflection

1. Have you ever felt the after-slump that happens when you've achieved the thing you've worked hard for? Were you surprised?

2. What coping mechanisms have you employed when going through big challenges? Upon reflection, do they serve you well now?

3. After you've reached a goal or made it through a traumatic experience, how do you reward yourself?

4. What skills has life's gritty times provided you with? How can those propel the adventures of your choosing?

Final Thoughts

Celebrate Yourself

Have you ever complimented a female friend about her accomplishment, who then scurries to downplay it?

"It was nothing." is at the tips of too many of our tongues. Like we're programmed somehow to resist affirmations.

For some of us whose achievements were highly celebrated during childhood, accepting compliments and celebrating our wins may come naturally. But for others, who because of past experiences or due to our gender training to stay small, we neglect to stop a moment and reflect.

To be clear, I'm often the non-celebrator of victories. "It took more than two decades to publish," I groaned when friends congratulated me on my first book.

The problem with minimizing the wins and pushing forward without acknowledging them is it leads to burnout. What's the point of doing the work if we're only going to double down on trudging ahead? We're making a bad habit of maximizing struggle, minimizing our effort.

Celebrate your accomplishments, whether it's a goal you've achieved or a challenge you've survived. Celebrate your efforts along the way, because it's not easy to inch forward toward progress. And if someone congratulates you, say "thank you." That's it. Thank you. No need to shrink yourself down by adding qualifiers. "Well, it was just...," or "I'm still struggling with __."

The only person whose validation you need is you.

Give Back

Sharing our stories is central to the healing journey. Writing or attending a peer-led group, or even a confidential social media support group can make all the difference. Knowing I wasn't unique or alone gave me a sense of security as I clawed my way through domestic abuse, divorce, and having my daughters kidnapped. They were terrible experiences I wouldn't wish on anyone. But when I listened to survivors of similar types of traumas, I felt bolstered. They'd made it through. There was an excellent possibility that I would too.

Immediately, I saw myself in give-back mode. It was okay to accept support, and one day, I would be in the position to give it. And it was in conjuring that image that helped me get comfortable reaching out for assistance when necessary.

Working as a domestic violence advocate was a great start. I gave up any 'woe is me, why am I so unlucky' due to a sense of mission.

Thirty subsequent years of working with people who've experienced intergenerational trauma and lots of crisis has reinforced this: Those who embrace that their hardship is a chance to help someone else down the line, or even amid their own predicament—so long as they're not tending to the needs of others to avoid dealing with their own issues—do better.

A book about giving, *Happy Money, the Science of Smarter Spending,* offers advice on finances that can be applied to donating your time.

Make sure the giving of yourself is a choice, not something you feel pushed to do. Make a connection. And know that you're making an impact, whether or not you see it right away.

Author Veronica Slaughter has seen her share of crises. Abducted by her abusive father and taken out of her birth country at the age of eight along with three siblings, it was four long years before she reunited with her mother. This trauma proved to be too much for her siblings to process, each dealing with their pain in different ways until they died prematurely. They had been her fortress, and then, they were gone. But Veronica had found meaning in healing others' pain. She became a chiropractor, then an author. "When I can help somebody, I feel better," she said. Her book about surviving international parental kidnapping exposed family secrets and aided younger generations of her relatives to gain empathy and context for their historical wounds. "When you reach back, it helps you."

Picture you, using your solid communication skills, building a strong community, using your stubborn persistence. Picture how great it will feel when you have the skills needed to scale whatever avalanche life dumps on you. Picture you, talking yourself off a ledge or quickly identifying who or what aid you'll need, and then resolving to get that help no matter what barriers threaten to make it impossible. Picture you, creating space for the adventures of your choosing. Picture you, reaching back to grab a hand that reaches up for yours when that next person who wants to know how to get through a similar challenge needs the help that only you can give.

Resources

Happy Money: The Science of Smarter Spending-Elizabeth Dunn and Michael Norton

Have You Seen These Children? A Memoir Veronica Slaughter

17. Conclusion

Conversations about trauma, resilience, and thriving after tough times are not in short supply. The message to "put the past behind you" is loud and clear.

But should we try to blot out our rough seasons? Ought we feel ashamed about things that happen to us?

Here's what I want you to get from this book:

Stuff happens to all of us. Some of us, more than others. There are factors which impact not only how often we experience chaos or trauma, but our access to resources to address it. It may feel like you're being singled out by God, The universe. Karma. Whatever you call it. I can almost guarantee you that you are not. And we do not automatically become stronger simply because we've survived. The passage of time does not bring healing if we've not done our due diligence to find, create, and/or accept the support needed to scale setbacks.

What I hope you've heard from me is that your challenges are nothing to be ashamed of. Old traumas and hurts need unpacking, but we need not blot them out of our memories. We incorporate them into our lives, gaining strength and support along the way, because we've chosen to be transformed rather than squashed by adversity.

We can dig deep. Show up for ourselves. Understand that getting support and services is part of the solution, and the very act of us following through is exponentially more important than what happens inside the asking. We can honestly assess our past with a vision for the future we're longing for.

We can calm the crazy that exists inside crises. We can increase times of serenity and know that when life happens hard again, we'll be ready.

You will always be your own best advocate. Learning to champion yourself rather than abdicating authority is an art form that can optimize other areas of your life.

When I learned to manage my emotions, for example, or write an effective email, or assertively communicate, it enhanced other areas. In my career. In my personal life. In the world. Taking skills I'd needed during hard times changed how I felt about my bumpy past, turning it from a source of shame to the origin of gain.

Your life is a story. You didn't write the beginning. The middle is in draft form. How it ends is not something you have complete control over, but you have the opportunity to influence it mightily.

You are grounded in grit.

Now, you've got more tools to turn your past challenges into your superpower.

GROUNDED IN GRIT: TURN YOUR CHALLENGES INTO SUPERPOWERS

Thank you for reading *Grounded in Grit*. Your honest review at online retailers will help me improve future editions and help shape other works.

Acknowledgements

Thank you to editors Margot Starbuck, Anna Katz, and to hyperspeller at wordrefiner.com. Thank you to Mark Leslie LeFebvre for being a terrific resource, and for referring me to Juan Padron for the book cover.

Thank you to We Love Memoirs and Barbara Bos at Women Writers, Womens Books, National Association of Memoir Writers, Gary Schwarz, and Dr.Virginia Simpson Burdt for your support.

Thank you to beta-readers Lloyd Russell, Joann Keder, Carol Krein, Terry Kirchener, and Marianne Hutchison.

Thank you to author Billi Jo Link and Ruth Quinlan for your support.

Special thank you to accountability buddy and formatter extraordinaire, author Joann Keder.

Massive thank you to dear family and friends, coworkers, readers of my first book, clients, podcast guests, and Patrons who helped make this book possible.

About Lizbeth Meredith

Lizbeth Meredith is a multi-award-winning author, speaker, podcast host of Persistence U with Lizbeth, and coach living in Chattanooga, Tennessee. Her memoir, *Pieces of Me: Rescuing My Kidnapped Daughters* is now a Lifetime TV movie, *Stolen by Their Father*.

A contributor to three anthologies including Chicken Soup for the Soul, Lizbeth has worked as a domestic violence advocate, a child abuse investigator, and retired after two decades as a juvenile probation supervisor.

Today, Lizbeth interviews crime victims and families for a true-crime channel and enjoys Facetime conversations with her adult daughters and grandpets.

Connect with Lizbeth

lameredith.com

Persistence U Podcast with Lizbeth

https://www.facebook.com/lizbethmeredithfan/

www.ingramcontent.com/pod-product-compliance
Lightning Source LLC
Chambersburg PA
CBHW022132080426
42734CB00006B/328